MW00397236

PUBLISHED ON THE FOUNDATION
ESTABLISHED IN MEMORY OF
JAMES WESLEY COOPER
OF THE CLASS OF 1865, YALE COLLEGE

SPEAKING WITH TONGUES

HISTORICALLY AND PSYCHOLOGICALLY
CONSIDERED

BY

GEORGE BARTON CUTTEN

PH.D., D.D., LL.D.

PRESIDENT OF COLGATE UNIVERSITY.

NEW HAVEN

YALE UNIVERSITY PRESS

LONDON · HUMPHREY MILFORD · OXFORD UNIVERSITY PRESS

1927

Printing Statement:

Due to the very old age and scarcity of this book, many of the pages may be hard to read due to the blurring of the original text, possible missing pages, missing text and other issues beyond our control.

Because this is such an important and rare work, we believe it is best to reproduce this book regardless of its original condition.

Thank you for your understanding.

THE

JAMES WESLEY COOPER

MEMORIAL PUBLICATION FUND

THE present volume is the ninth work published by the Yale University Press on the James Wesley Cooper Memorial Publication Fund. This Foundation was established March 30, 1918, by a gift to Yale University from Mrs. Ellen H. Cooper in memory of her husband, Rev. James Wesley Cooper, D.D., who died in New York City, March 16, 1916. Dr. Cooper was a member of the Class of 1865, Yale College, and for twenty-five years pastor of the South Congregational Church of New Britain, Connecticut. For thirty years he was a corporate member of the American Board of Commissioners for Foreign Missions and from 1885 until the time of his death was a Fellow of Yale University, serving on the Corporation as one of the Successors of the Original Trustees.

CONTENTS

PREFACE

THERE are two adequate treatises on the subject of speaking with tongues, viz.: E. Lombard, *De la Glossolalia chez les premiers chrètiens et des phénomènes similaires,* and E. Mosiman, *Das Zungenreden, geschichtlich und psychologisch untersucht.* Unfortunately, while numerous articles have been written on the subject, there is no book available to English readers which covers the ground. To supply this need is the purpose of this book.

In only one instance, in the books which I have published, have I made any pretense to a scholarly production. In all other cases I have professedly had the general reader in mind during the preparation. While I have used the latest results of scholarly research, I have tried to interpret these results to those unfamiliar with technical subleties, and to evaluate them for the general reader.

It is the latter plan which has been followed in the present book. There have been many claims made for the phenomena of speaking with tongues, and much technical disputing, especially on New Testament interpretation and psychological explanation. While finding it profitable to use the material connected with these technical disagreements, in both cases I have tried to simplify and to articulate it so as to make available that portion not readily grasped by those unfamiliar with Greek exegesis or technical psychological terms.

The plan of the book is to present the historical material first, using that connected with the Christian church, which has been the chief inspiration of the phenomena, although they are not unknown in other religions. One chapter has been devoted to non-religious speaking with tongues, and the final chapter to psychological explanation.

The only originality claimed for this book is that of selection, which, after all, is the most important factor in originality.

I wish to express my appreciation of the privilege of using the material found in the books and articles listed in the bibliography, from some of which I have quoted so freely, and especially do I appreciate the use of the three illustrations taken from *From India to the Planet Mars.*

GEORGE BARTON CUTTEN

Colgate University,
   Hamilton, New York.

SPEAKING WITH TONGUES

SPEAKING WITH TONGUES

SPEAKING with tongues is an experience which
most people believe to be confined to apostolic
times and bestowed as a special favor on a few followers of the crucified Jesus. The church as a whole
seems to have looked upon it as a miracle performed
to meet the exigencies of a special situation, and
which, in a less important way, was continued to
meet other peculiar problems, but was soon discon-
tinued. On the other hand, there are not wanting
hundreds and thousands of people who are willing
to testify that they have heard or experienced this
phenomenon in our present day, and many empha-
size the importance of the experience in religious development and in personal consecration.

The distinction which has been made between the
accounts of the marvel, as given in the Acts of the
Apostles by Luke and in the First Letter to the
Corinthians by Paul, is most necessary, for all the
modern cases follow the Pauline type. This is a comparatively definite type and fairly well understood
by modern psychology. Just what took place at

Pentecost is not clear from the account, and so far as we know has never been duplicated, if we take the account at its face value. The confusion between the two forms arises from the fact that they are called by the same name. This might lead us to think that the phenomena were originally the same, but that some changes have been made in the narrative describing one of them.

If we are to trace the history of this experience down to the present time, why should we not also see if it cannot be traced in the other direction? We could, I believe, find examples which would as clearly indicate its appearance long before the days of Christianity. Were records as numerous and as amplified, there seems little doubt that it could be traced to primitive times, for it is a primitive experience, a reverberation of very early days in the history of the race.

There are some phenomena recorded in the Old Testament which are evidently the products of ecstasy, but which are there classed under the head of prophecy. In the New Testament there is a differentiation between prophecy and speaking with tongues. Both the prophet and the glossolalic delivered their messages in ecstasy and both considered themselves possessed by a divine spirit while thus employed. Psychologically the states were the same, and one was apt to run into the other. An ecstatic might begin his message in prophecy and end with speaking with tongues; this happened very frequently. Prophecy was delivered in words which could be understood, speaking in tongues consisted of meaningless syllables; otherwise there was probably no psychological distinction.

The prophet was the mouthpiece of God, and as such would not unlikely use a strange tongue at times. There are some things which seem to connect the Old Testament ecstasy of the prophets with that of the tongues of the New Testament, although we must recognize that the prophet sometimes declared an understandable message in a very direct way to those to whom he believed Jehovah had sent him. Saul among the prophets became another man, and in different places the record shows that the prophets were considered mad; in the New Testament glossolalics were called drunken. The prophesying of the priests of Baal was described as shouting, leaping, and self-mutilation, and the fact that the various messengers which Saul sent to take David began to prophesy, group by group, when they saw and heard the prophets, shows that the phenomenon was contagious. Isaiah referred to those who had familiar spirits and to those who were wizards as persons who "chirp and mutter." The particular expression which ecstasy will take at any one time is a matter of suggestion quite largely, and the fact that the Old

3

Testament prophets danced (as Saul did) and acted in other ways which showed instability, and that the New Testament glossolalics spoke in unintelligible language is a matter of slight difference in the motor manifestation of ecstasy.

For a modern man to permit himself to indulge in this form of expression means that he must put himself in a psychological state where the controlling apparatus of his mind is not functioning, and where the primitive reactions, which usually sleep in the subconscious, find their way to the surface and represent the individual.

Thinking is a comparatively late development of the human mind, and for many people is, except in a rudimentary way, a task too heavy for the mental machine. Vocal expression, on the other hand, is a very early reaction. In the lowest forms of mammals it consists of a definite sound or series of sounds emitted as a reaction to a certain experience. The urge for vocal expression seems to increase as we ascend in the scale of animal life, until real speech is developed. This was one of the great steps in advance made by our pre-human or early human ancestors, and, following this, development was more rapid. In monkeys there seems to be an impulse toward continual vocal expression, without much relation to conveying any meaning.

With thinking as a late development and a difficult attainment, thought processes are usually not of long duration, and any attempt to prolong them ends in the blocking of the process. On the other hand, vocal utterance was so early developed in the race and so firmly ingrained in our nervous system that it is carried on with greatest ease. This utterance may be language or simply a series of sounds; the latter is more primitive and consequently more easily sustained than the former. Keeping in mind the race history in connection with these two human functions, it may be seen that, when a person stands up to speak, it is not the utterance but the thinking, back of the utterance, which causes the strain. With those who find even rudimentary thought difficult, speech of an intelligent nature cannot long progress, the thinking process soon refusing to function; and when, owing to the ease of operation and the suggestion to action, speech continues after thought is exhausted, a series of meaningless syllables results. This is the Pauline type of speaking with tongues.

In addition to the difficulty of thinking, due to the fact that the organism is not yet adjusted to the comparatively new function, there are certain circumstances which aggravate the task and bring about more rapidly a cessation of thought. One of the most powerful of these is excitement. Speaking more or less figuratively, we say that during excitement there is an excessive pressure of nervous

5

energy, and at such times this energy tends to be diverted from the less used and less easily traversed paths into the paths of more frequent and less difficult discharge. The latter are naturally those which have been for thousands and perhaps millions of years the usual paths of discharge, such as the instinctive reactions which we have inherited from our primitive or pre-human ancestors.

It is evident, then, that the emotional energy generated by excitement tends to inhibit thought and to facilitate some primitive reaction which the circumstances suggest. It is noticeable that not only at Corinth, and at Jerusalem on the day of Pentecost, but in the examples which these modern days present to us, speaking with tongues comes only under especially exciting circumstances, such as during revival services. In our time it has been vouchsafed almost always, if not entirely, to those of low mental ability. Persons of high ability, whose nervous energy would more easily flow into channels of thought, have sought the gift in vain.

In addition to excitement and low mentality, one other factor is likely to be present in those who speak in tongues, and that is illiteracy. The illiterate naturally have poor power of expression and a limited vocabulary. When the excessive energy presses for discharge, the appropriate words are not forthcoming, and at first primitive cries and later mean-

6

ingless syllables take their place. When we have, then, these three elements and added to them the power of suggestion and expectancy, we can prognosticate speaking with tongues as a result. We must not, however, at this time anticipate the psychological explanation which will be the subject of the last chapter.

There is no reason for us to think that the modern examples of speaking with tongues are fundamentally different from the experiences which caused Paul so much worry at Corinth. Human nature has not changed either in power or in fundamental elements in the last two millenniums. We can, therefore, be fairly certain that in investigating and describing and explaining the modern manifestations, we are, at the same time, helping to explain the phenomena which the apostle tried to control. His apostolic position put him in a more favorable place from which to exercise authority than anyone holds today; but, on the other hand, we are armed with a scientific explanation which he lacked. It is doubtful, however, if our explanation will be any more successful than his authority in restraining the manifestation.

None of the large Christian denominations now attempts to cultivate this experience. As a rule those who seek to speak with tongues are in small, isolated congregations. They lay emphasis upon the gift of the Holy Spirit and his manifestation here among men, and they naturally turn to the Day of Pentecost and the attendant marvels. By these persons the Spirit is supposed to be manifested only to a favored few, not because of a limit to his power or his willingness, but because the great mass of those who call themselves Christians are lacking in the consecration which such a gift presupposes. Anyone, they say, may receive this gift if he will fulfil the conditions. Not infrequently coupled with the gift of tongues is that of miraculous healing, both being manifestations of the indwelling of the Holy Spirit, according to the teaching of these groups.

Perhaps we should not be far out of the way in affirming that there has been no time since the Day of Pentecost when the gift has been more sought than in the present century, with the possible exception of the time when Paul wrote to the Corinthians. We find relatively few manifestations during the days of the early church and especially few in the Middle Ages. This is the more remarkable since at that time the unusual and the miraculous were emphasized in the religious world, and an appeal to the marvellous was one of the chief proofs of the reality and value of the Christian life. Even the few cases we have do not bear the earmarks of genuineness.

To account for this absence or scarcity of manifestation, there were at least two factors. In the first place, manifestations of this kind were confused with others, or were, perhaps, called by the name of other religious experiences. There was, on the one hand, prophecy, which was usually delivered in an ecstatic state, and, on the other hand, what was called demoniacal possession, tapering off into witchcraft. It can well be seen how speaking with tongues might be confused with such phenomena. In the second place, the Middle Ages were times in which solitude and humility were especially characteristic of Christianity, and speaking with tongues, which is an exceedingly showy gift, would not be sought or welcomed by the enthusiasts of that time. The anchorites in the desert would naturally not speak with tongues, for there would be no one to whom to speak, and monks and potential saints who were spending their time in all sorts of self-inflicted torture to mortify the flesh would eschew such bombastic manifestations.

There seems to be little difference in nationalities regarding the frequency of the gift, for it is regulated more by individual psychology than by racial traits. Perhaps more important than either was the current preaching, and the consequent obligation to cultivate such experiences. The suggestion and expectancy, designated above as important factors in producing the phenomena, were potent regardless of race or nationality, provided, of course, there were among the hearers those to whom such a gift appealed as a test of spiritual favor.

It would be difficult, if not impossible, to find a more useless gift. Paul recognized its lack of value and expressed himself concerning it in no uncertain way. Subsequent experience has confirmed his estimate, for at no time since he wrote has it been of practical value, unless we can designate as such the leading of people to think that they are especially favored of God by becoming instruments of such a manifestation. To the contrary, it has probably been a detriment to pure religion, because it has furnished as a test for religious worth abnormal psychological experiences rather than a changed or an improved life. To the great majority of people in this practical age it provides no appeal, and, in fact, it never has appealed except to a very few.

The few with whom the gift has found favor have been encouraged to develop it by the promises recorded in the last few verses of the Gospel of Mark, a portion of scripture which modern commentators regard as a late addition. The proof of the Spirit's presence, which it seems to give, and the successes which have attended efforts in this direction have also been encouraging. As a result the present manifestations are apparently not diminishing, but will probably decrease as knowledge accumulates, and as natural inhibition and control develop.

CHAPTER II

NEW TESTAMENT

THE following are the references to speaking
with tongues in the New Testament:

Acts 2:

4 And they were all filled with the Holy Spirit, and
began to speak with other tongues, as the Spirit gave
them utterance.

5 Now there were dwelling at Jerusalem Jews, devout
men, from every nation under heaven. 6 And when this
sound was heard, the multitude came together, and were
confounded, because that every man heard them speaking
in his own language. 7 And they were all amazed and
marvelled, saying, Behold, are not all these that speak
Galilæans? 8 And how hear we, every man in our own
language wherein we were born? 9 Parthians and Medes
and Elamites, and the dwellers in Mesopotamia, in Judæa
and Cappadocia, in Pontus and Asia, 10 in Phrygia and
Pamphylia, in Egypt and the parts of Libya about Cy-
rene, and sojourners from Rome, both Jews and prose-
lytes, 11 Cretans and Arabians, we hear them speaking
in our tongues the mighty works of God. 12 And they
were all amazed, and were perplexed, saying one to another, What meaneth this? 13 But others mocking said,
They are filled with new wine.

14 But Peter, standing up with the eleven, lifted up his
voice, and spake forth unto them, *saying*, Ye men of
Judæa, and all ye that dwell at Jerusalem, be this known
unto you, and give ear unto my words. 15 For these are

not drunken, as ye suppose; seeing it is *but* the third
hour of the day; 16 but this is that which hath been
spoken through the prophet Joel:

17 And it shall be in the last days, saith God,
I will pour forth of my Spirit upon all flesh:
And your sons and your daughters shall prophesy,
And your young men shall see visions,
And your old men shall dream dreams:

18 Yea and on my servants and on my handmaidens in
those days
Will I pour forth of my Spirit; and they shall
prophesy.

19 And I will show wonders in the heaven above,
And signs on the earth beneath;
Blood, and fire, and vapor of smoke:

20 The sun shall be turned into darkness,
And the moon into blood,
Before the day of the Lord come,
That great and notable *day:*

21 And it shall be, that whosoever shall call on the name
of the Lord shall be saved.

Acts 10:

44 While Peter yet spake these words, the Holy Spirit
fell on all them that heard the word. 45 And they of the
circumcision that believed were amazed, as many as came
with Peter, because that on the Gentiles also was poured
out the gift of the Holy Spirit. 46 For they heard them
speak with tongues, and magnify God.

Acts 19:

6 And when Paul had laid his hands upon them, the
Holy Spirit came on them; and they spake with tongues,
and prophesied.

I Cor. 12:

10 And to another workings of miracles; and to another prophecy; and to another discernings of spirits; to another *divers* kinds of tongues; and to another the interpretation of tongues: 28 And God hath set some in the church, first apostles, secondly prophets, thirdly teachers, then miracles, then gifts of healings, helps, governments, *divers* kinds of tongues. 29 Are all apostles? are all prophets? are all teachers? are all *workers of* miracles? 30 have all gifts of healings? do all speak with tongues? do all interpret?

I Cor. 13:

If I speak with the tongues of men and of angels, but have not love, I am become sounding brass, or a clanging cymbal. 8 Love never faileth: but whether *there be* prophecies, they shall be done away; whether *there be* tongues, they shall cease; whether *there be* knowledge, it shall be done away.

I Cor. 14:

Follow after love; yet desire earnestly spiritual *gifts*, but rather that ye may prophesy. 2 For he that speaketh in a tongue speaketh not unto men, but unto God; for no man understandeth; but in the spirit he speaketh mysteries. 3 But he that prophesieth speaketh unto men edification, and exhortation, and consolation. 4 He that speaketh in a tongue edifieth himself; but he that prophesieth edifieth the church. 5 Now I would have you all speak with tongues, but rather that ye should prophesy: and greater is he that prophesieth than he that speaketh with tongues, except he interpret, that the church may receive edifying. 6 But now, brethren, if I come unto you speaking with tongues, what shall I profit you, unless I speak to you either by way of revelation, or of knowledge, or of prophesying, or of teaching? 7 Even things without life, giving a voice, whether pipe or harp, if they give not a distinction in the sounds, how shall it be known what is piped or harped? 8 For if the trumpet give an uncertain voice, who shall prepare himself for war? 9 So also ye, unless ye utter by the tongue speech easy to be understood, how shall it be known what is spoken? for ye will be speaking into the air. 10 There are, it may be, so many kinds of voices in the world, and no *kind* is without signification. 11 If then I know not the meaning of the voice, I shall be to him that speaketh a barbarian, and he that speaketh will be a barbarian unto me. 12 So also ye, since ye are zealous of spiritual *gifts,* seek that ye may abound unto the edifying of the church. 13 Wherefore let him that speaketh in a tongue pray that he may interpret. 14 For if I pray in a tongue, my spirit prayeth, but my understanding is unfruitful. 15 What is it then? I will pray with the spirit, and I will pray with the understanding also: I will sing with the spirit, and I will sing with the understanding also. 16 Else if thou bless with the spirit, how shall he that filleth the place of the unlearned say the Amen at thy giving of thanks, seeing he knoweth not what thou sayest? 17 For thou verily givest thanks well, but the other is not edified. 18 I thank God, I speak with tongues more than you all: 19 howbeit in the church I had rather speak five words with my understanding, that I might instruct others also, than ten thousand words in a tongue.

20 Brethren, be not children in mind: yet in malice be ye babes, but in mind be men. 21 In the law it is written, By men of strange tongues and by the lips of strangers

will I speak unto this people; and not even thus will they hear me, saith the Lord. 22 Wherefore tongues are for a sign, not to them that believe, but to the unbelieving: but prophesying *is for a sign,* not to the unbelieving, but to them that believe. 23 If therefore the whole church be assembled together and all speak with tongues, and there come in men unlearned or unbelieving, will they not say that ye are mad? 24 But if all prophesy, and there come in one unbelieving or unlearned, he is reproved by all, he is judged by all; 25 the secrets of his heart are made manifest; and so he will fall down on his face and worship God, declaring that God is among you indeed.

26 What is it then, brethren? When ye come together, each one hath a psalm, hath a teaching, hath a revelation, hath a tongue, hath an interpretation. Let all things be done unto edifying. 27 If any man speaketh in a tongue, *let it be* by two, or at the most three, and *that* in turn; and let one interpret: 28 but if there be no interpreter, let him keep silence in the church; and let him speak to himself, and to God. 29 And let the prophets speak *by* two or three, and let the others discern. 30 But if a revelation be made to another sitting by, let the first keep silence. 31 For ye all can prophesy one by one, that all may learn, and all may be exhorted; 32 and the spirits of the prophets are subject to the prophets; 33 for God is not *a God* of confusion, but of peace.

As in all the churches of the saints, 34 let the women keep silence in the churches: for it is not permitted unto them to speak; but let them be in subjection, as also saith the law. 35 And if they would learn anything, let them ask their own husbands at home: for it is shameful for a woman to speak in the church. 36 What? was it from you that the word of God went forth? or came it unto you alone?

37 If any man thinketh himself to be a prophet, or spiritual, let him take knowledge of the things which I write unto you, that they are the commandment of the Lord. 38 But if any man is ignorant, let him be ignorant.

39 Wherefore, my brethren, desire earnestly to prophesy, and forbid not to speak with tongues. 40 But let all things be done decently and in order.

Mark 16:

17 And these signs shall accompany them that believe: in my name shall they cast out demons; they shall speak with new tongues.

What was meant by the phenomenon "speaking with tongues" was evidently not clear, if we can judge by the different New Testament accounts, and in the first century there was no unanimity of opinion concerning either the value or the definition of the marvel. The general understanding of this term is that taken from a superficial reading of the second chapter of the Acts of the Apostles; namely, that illiterate Galileans spoke in many different foreign languages without previous training.

St. Cyril affirmed that "they spoke with language which they had never learnt, and thus was fulfilled the prophecy: 'There is neither speech nor language but their voices are heard among them,'" to say the least, an incorrect rendering of Ps. 19: 3. Gregory

Nazianzen said, "So they spoke with foreign tongues and not with their native tongues, and great was the wonder, the word being preached by them who had not learned." Jerome explained the miracle by saying, "In order that being about to preach to many nations, they might receive different kinds of tongues"; but we have no evidence of their ever using the gift in that way. St. Chrysostom and St. Augustine insisted that "the miracle of Pentecost is the antithesis of the confusion of tongues at Babel. There the one language had been divided into many; here the many languages were united in one man." Gregory of Nyssa elaborated the idea by saying that the power of universal communication was lost at the earthly building of the tower, and was restored in the spiritual building of the church. There is not the slightest evidence for this. The hearers were expressly designated as Jews, and the enumeration given was not of languages but of countries. The most that can possibly be taken from this account, so far as the apostles are concerned, is that the differences of dialect, of Greek or Aramaic, were eliminated; and the wonder is that this should be so when the speakers were Galileans, who would naturally be supposed to have such a pronounced dialect.

A more careful reading of the passage will show that Luke seems to affirm that the miracle did not lie in the tongues of the speakers, but in the ears of the hearers. One prominent modern historian (Dr. Schaff) has accepted this view. He thinks that although the apostle spoke in unintelligible ecstatic utterances, similar to the phenomenon which Paul described in his letter to the Corinthians, the Spirit interpreted the utterances to those present, each one of whom thought he heard in his own language. The very phrase, "Speaking with a tongue," shows, however, that it was considered that the miracle lay in the tongue of the speaker and not in the ear of the hearer. Both Gregory Nazianzen and Jerome thought of the miracle as one of speech and not of hearing. Certainly, though, the claim that the apostles received this gift so as to enable them, unlettered as they were, to speak to the different nations to which they had been sent, does not seem to be a valid one; we never hear of their using it in missionary work, and, indeed, the prevalence of the Greek language made this entirely unnecessary. Peter does not refer to the use of a foreign language when he defends the disciples on a charge of drunkenness, although that would have been a valuable argument.

One commentator goes so far as to say that "the sudden communication of a faculty of speaking foreign languages is neither logically possible nor psychologically and morally conceivable."[1] Luke does not even seem to be consistent with himself, for in his

[1] H. A. W. Meyer, *Commentary of Acts,* 2:4.

18

two other references to this phenomenon he evidently refers to the same kind of experiences which Paul describes. In both these cases (Acts 10: 44-46, 19: 6), the plain statement is made that the apostles "spoke with tongues," evidently referring to the fact that they broke out in ecstatic speech and glorified God, but in his Pentecostal account the term "other" tongues was used. This is unique; it marks the first realization and reception of Christianity, and it does not seem as though this phenomenon were a part of normal worship. The experience at Pentecost differs from these two cases and the Corinthian phenomena in three ways; namely, in the first incident there was a "sound of the rushing of a mighty wind," tongues parting asunder as of fire were seen, and the apostles began to speak with other tongues and were understood by men of other dialects without the aid of an interpreter.

Notwithstanding the fact that the Epistle to the Ephesians is supposed to have been a circular letter, it would seem from Eph. 5: 18 and 19, where Paul exhorts the Ephesians not to be drunk with wine, wherein is riot, but to be filled with the spirit, speaking to themselves in psalms and hymns and spiritual songs, that the Ephesians had knowledge and experience in speaking with tongues other than that recorded in Acts and to which we have just referred. Paul witnessed the early experience in Ephesus and wrote his epistles to the Corinthians from there, and it is not unlikely that the phenomenon was somewhat common in that city. Again, in Col. 3: 16, he exhorts the Colossians to admonish themselves with "prayers and hymns and spiritual songs," using the same language as when writing to the Ephesians; and in I Thess. 5: 19 and 20 he says, "Quench not the Spirit, despise not prophesyings." Since the chief spiritual gift was speaking with tongues, while prophesying, also a spiritual gift, was referred to separately, it looks as though the apostle referred to the gift of tongues, when he exhorted them not to quench the Spirit. If these are references to tongues, as seems likely, then the gift of tongues was not confined to Corinth, but was somewhat widespread, as indeed we should expect it to be. All of these cases were evidently the same kind that Paul knew well at Corinth, and the phenomena were so well known and so well defined as to require no description or comment. The Pentecostal experience, then, stands out alone—differing from those at Cæsarea, Ephesus, Colossæ, Thessalonica, and Corinth; and yet it is called by the same name as though it were identical with them. It has been suggested that perhaps the glamor surrounding the early church and the influence of the attendant wonders—the wind and the tongues of fire—account for Luke's misunderstanding of the first appearance of this gift. Zaugg gives another explanation: he thinks that the form which the account of the Pentecostal experience took was occasioned, not on account of Luke's ignorance of speaking with tongues, but because he wished to make the experience at Pentecost correspond to the giving of the law at Sinai when, according to a Midrash of the ninth century, "Although the ten commandments were announced with a single sound, yet all the people heard the voices; i.e., all the nations of the world heard God in their own languages."[1]

Paul's reference to tongues in the fourteenth chapter of First Corinthians is very different from Luke's description of the Pentecostal experience. Origen says that Paul says of himself he is debtor both to the Greek and barbarian (Rom. 1: 14), and how then is he debtor to all? By speaking the language of each of them. He then quotes Paul as saying, "I speak more with tongues of you all" (I Cor. 14: 18), a rendering which the Greek makes possible, but which the context forbids. Chrysostom says of I Cor. 12-14, "The whole of this passage is extremely obscure," and so it is, in view of his interpretation of Acts 2. Practically all modern commentators recognize a decided difference between Luke's Pentecostal description, and that of Paul in his letter to the Corinthians.

[1] E. H. Zaugg, *A Genetic Study of the Spirit Phenomena in the New Testament.*

It seems that when Paul was in Ephesus in the spring of the year 57, he received a letter from the Christian community of Corinth asking his precise instructions concerning embarrassing subjects. One of the questions concerned spiritual gifts or perhaps better translated, "the inspired." The apostle considered it sufficiently important to reply by a series of considerations and instructions, found in chapters 12-14, which he introduced in these terms, "On the subject of the inspired, brethren, I do not wish you to remain in ignorance." In other words, "It will be better for me to enlighten your judgment on these matters, for I see you have need of it."[1]

The life of primitive churches gravitated around the phenomena of inspiration, and there were good reasons why Corinthians should be especially interested in this subject. "It was a gift congenial to the Corinthian temperament. They were well accustomed to the idea of the divinity speaking through the lips of human priest or priestess, who, when seized by the power and inspiration of the God were plunged into a state of unconscious ecstasy, and so, in frenzy, delivered the oracular reply."[2] They were familiar with persons from whom the gods had removed the mind and spoke through the soulless body. They had known persons similar to Paul's description of

[1] E. Lombard, *De la glossolalia, etc.*, p. 1.
[2] D. Walker, *The Gift of Tongues*, p. 65.

22

himself (I Cor. 14: 14) so filled with Divine power that the mind was rendered unfruitful.

There was a certain number of faculties or gifts which, by their extraordinary character or extraordinary development, were supposed to portray the heart of the church, and which, among individuals in whom they were manifested, revealed the presence and efficacious action of the Spirit. These gifts, of which we have partial enumerations, but not a systematic and complete catalogue, were very different and also diversely appreciated; so that finally they resulted in jealousies, competitions, and personal rivalries. The one above all others which excited the admiration and ambitious emulation of the Corinthians was speaking in tongues, or "glossolalia." One may deduce from the expression (14: 49), "Forbid not that one speak in tongues," that the gift had its enemies, but undoubtedly most of the Corinthians coveted it. At Corinth the question of inspiration was the question of speaking with tongues. Paul, evidently conforming to their language, said, "If anyone think himself to be a prophet or inspired" (14: 37), and throughout the chapter it is this gift of tongues which is compared with prophecy (3-6, 22, 25, 27-33). Paul does not describe the phenomenon, as the facts with which he deals were evidently well known to his readers. Glossolalic himself in a very high degree, this circumstance does not remove from him the liberty of critical appreciation in regard to this gift, but, on the other hand, confers on his criticism a value and a peculiar interest.

To him, speaking in tongues appeared as a language of which the man was not the author but the organ of expression. He said (I Cor. 14: 14), "If I pray in a tongue, my spirit prayeth, but my understanding is unfruitful." "My spirit" here may mean "the divine spirit which inspires me." When thus inspired he considered that the intelligence was in abeyance. Philo said, "In us intelligence is banished by the invasion of the divine spirit; if the latter retires, it returns." Is not Paul expressing Philo's idea? The words used in speaking with tongues did not appear to come from him, and may thus be directly attributed to an independent spirit possessing him, the dynamic manifestations of which were looked upon as most precious and most convincing. For this reason it seems that the marvel was produced not only for the believing community but for non-Christian attendants also. It should be noted, however, that, like the prophets, the glossolalics did not address their fellow-men but spoke to God (I Cor. 14: 28). Thus Paul says he will pray with the spirit and he will pray with the understanding, the former was worshipping God and the latter was edifying the church; so in the church he would rather speak five words with the understanding so that he might in-

24

struct others than ten thousand words in a tongue. At the same time he thanked God that he spoke in tongues more than others, for this was worship.

Paul warns them, "If the whole Church be assembled together and all speak with tongues, and there come in men unlearned and unbelieving, will they not say that you are mad?" (I Cor. 14: 23). This text in connection with others where he exhorts them to "speak only one at a time" and to "let all things be done decently and in order" shows that in Paul's time, as in modern times, speaking with tongues was accompanied by other motor automatisms which gave the impression of unbalanced minds. The effect of Pentecost upon unsympathetic hearers does not seem to have been very different, for there the disciples were charged with being drunken. Scenes similar to those suggested by Paul's and Luke's references are not uncommon in some modern revival and camp meetings, and from descriptions given of them we can comprehend Paul's anxiety about affairs at Corinth.

It is evident that Paul considered the gift of tongues of use to the individual in worship, or for his own edification, and not for the instruction of the hearers, for the latter could not understand these utterances without an interpreter. In his enumeration of spiritual gifts in the twelfth chapter of First Corinthians he puts "tongues" in the last place.

"Though they might speak with the tongues of men and of angels, if they were without that love which does not behave itself unseemly, they were only sounding brass or a clanging cymbal." He compares the gift of tongues to the notes of a pipe or harp, without distinction of sounds. In his experience, people were not hearing in their own languages, but just the opposite: no one could understand a word.

Paul advised against the use of this gift in assemblies, on account of its being unintelligible. It was anti-fraternal, for those who did not speak had no part in the service. He told them they might give very good thanks, but the auditors could not respond with "Amen" to the thanks, because they did not know what was said. For this reason they were not edified, and every hearer became a foreigner. Paul, therefore, compared tongues with prophecy, the latter being for the benefit and edification of the hearer. What was true of the hearer was also true of the speaker, for neither one understood a word. To Paul the lack on the part of the hearers was more objectionable than that on the part of the speaker, for the latter had an exaltation which was considered beneficial.

It is to be noted, further, that Paul compared and opposed speaking with tongues to prophecy, to knowledge, to all comprehensible and reasonable discourse (14: 6, 19 ff.), and not to the mother-tongue of the

26

inspired one. The only "interpretation" of which he spoke was one which proceeded from a charismatic privilege, since it would be natural, if it had to do with ordinary languages, to foresee the simple eventuality of a translation given by some polyglot attendant. Further, if these were languages unknown to the speaker but which were spoken by others, which the glossolalics unseasonably employed, how can we conceive that Paul would order them to reserve this gift for private edification, in place of saying to them to await an opportunity to edify foreigners?

Paul's description of the gift has been thus epitomized: "It was evidently frenzied or ecstatic utterances of sounds ordinarily unintelligible both to speakers and to hearers, except such as might be endowed by the Holy Spirit with a special gift of interpretation. The speaker was supposed to be completely under the control of the Spirit, to be a mere passive instrument in His hands, and to be moved and played upon by Him. His utterances were not his own but the utterances of the Spirit, and he was commonly unconscious of what he was saying." The gift was considered most spiritual because the speaker had less control of himself, but its real value must be computed by its worth to others. Although it was the most showy of all gifts, it was of little value and must not be exercised, said the apostle, unless

27

an interpreter were present. The words were divine
and not human, and had evidently no relation to
any human tongue, so that the speaker was thought
to be demented. Paul thought of it as futile for progress and useless for believers. It is really a high testimony to Paul's common sense, mystic as he was,
that in those days, when every one extolled the abnormal and regarded it as "spiritual," he had sufficient perspicacity to determine the insignificant value
of speaking with tongues. Had the gift changed in
character within half a century, were there two different phenomena included under the same term, or
was either Luke or Paul mistaken in his description?

Another explanation comes in another work. The
writer affirms that, according to the old view of
speaking with tongues, interpretation was not necessary, and according to the new view interpretation
was impossible. His theory is intended to harmonize
the accounts of Luke and Paul, and to provide a
place for interpretation. The modern view, he says,
does not account for the words of Luke, "Are not all
these that speak Galileans! And how hear we them
every one in his own language, wherein we were
born?" Accordingly he opines that the utterances
were spoken in ecstasy, in harmony with the modern
view, but were really other languages. The speaker
did not know the language and was unconscious of
what he was saying, and when the ecstasy was over

he did not remember what he had said.[1] He accounts
for this in a rational manner, by the well-known
phenomenon of the abnormally exalted memory in
certain ecstatic cases. Conditions for hearing other
languages were present both at Jerusalem and at Corinth. Jews from all parts of the known world were
constantly returning to Jerusalem, as for example at
this time of Pentecost, and Corinth was a cosmo-
politan city.

There were two other gifts closely connected with
the gift of tongues, they were the interpretation of
tongues and the discerning of spirits. In Paul's list
the discerning of spirits precedes that of speaking
with tongues, which in turn precedes the interpretation of tongues. It is evident that at that time as well
as in later experience, it was considered possible for
evil spirits to control persons and perform wonders
similar to those performed by good spirits, and
among the gifts of both classes of spirits was that of
tongues. In the Middle Ages demons were charged
with counterfeiting the gifts of the Spirit. It may
have been that the more cultured portion of the Corinthian church thought that the gift of tongues was
the result of demoniacal possession similar to that
which they had seen among the heathen around
them, and they therefore tried to stop it. Paul found
it necessary to restrain them and to tell them (I Cor.

[1] A. Wright, *Some New Testament Problems.*

14: 39) that they must forbid not to speak with tongues. As far as some of these gifts were concerned it was indeed difficult for them to discern the spirit, but by the other actions the discerning must be done. The interpretation of tongues seems to be a gift not unlike that of tongues itself and will be discussed later.

Since the close of apostolic times, commentators have been concerned with Pentecost and the tongues episode, and have tried in some way to give a rational explanation, especially in connection with Paul's account in the first letter to the Corinthians. Mosiman has collected a number of interpretations based on the different meanings of the word "Glossa."[1] The word is used in Greek in three different senses; namely, (1) the physical organ, and is used in this sense by Paul in I Cor. 14: 9; (2) in the sense of a language; and (3) referring to a previous or obsolete expression. Interpretations of the gift have been made using each one of these meanings as a basis, although the second meaning, that of a language, is the most common use and is the most frequent foundation of commentators. There seems to be little doubt that both in Luke's and in Paul's account this is the meaning used. It is to be noted that the older commentators take the Pente-

[1] E. Mosiman, *Das Zungenreden, geschichtlich und psychologisch untersucht*, p. 21 ff.

30

costal experience as a basis and endeavor to reconcile Paul's account with it, but the modern commentators take Paul's account as a basis, largely because all later cases conform to this form, and try to reconcile Luke's account with it. Paul's account is taken as a basis for other reasons; namely, because it is earlier and written by an eye-witness.

CHAPTER III

FATHERS AND SAINTS

AFTER Paul's damning glossolalia by faint praise when writing to the Corinthian Church, it seems not to have taken a conspicuous place among the spiritual gifts. In fact Dr. Middleton[1] has gone so far as to say that "after the apostolic times, there is not, in all history, one instance, either well attested, or even so much as mentioned, of any particular person who had ever exercised that gift [of tongues], or pretended to exercise it in any age or country whatever." As we shall soon see, this is far from true, yet it shows how insignificant has been the development of the gift which characterized the advent of the Christian Church.

The subsequent references to it are both infrequent and obscure. It is sometimes difficult from the accounts given to distinguish this gift from that of prophecy. For example, Irenæus (130-202 A.D.), when speaking of Marcus the heretic, describes a scene in which Marcus tells a woman to open her mouth, speak whatever occurs to her, and she shall prophesy. "She then vainly puffed up and elated by these words, and greatly excited in soul by the expectation that it is herself that is to prophesy, her

---

[1] *Inquiry into Miraculous Powers*, p. 120.

heart beating violently (from emotion), reaches the requisite pitch of audacity, and idly, as well as imprudently, utters some nonsense as it happens to occur to her, such as might be expected from one heated by an empty spirit."[1] It will be seen that this is not very different from the phenomenon in the Church at Corinth, and from that manifested since that time.

Irenæus has a more definite reference, however. He said (V, 6, 1): "When the Apostle says, 'We speak wisdom among the perfect,' by 'the perfect' he means those who had received the Spirit of God, and in all tongues speak through the Spirit of God, as he himself also spake. As also we (now) hear many brethren in the Church having prophetic gifts, and speaking in all sorts of languages through the Spirit, and bringing to open day the hidden things of men for edification, and expounding the mysteries of God, whom the Apostle calls spiritual." The word translated "diverse" or "all sorts of" is somewhat obscure and does not occur elsewhere. It is not certain, then, whether he means that these brethren spoke foreign languages or the peculiar utterance to which Paul refers. At any rate it was of no practical value to Irenæus since he was compelled to learn the language of Gaul. There is no reason, however, for not

---

[1] Roberts and Donaldson, *Ante-Nicene Fathers*, I, p. 334.

taking seriously the words, "We hear m ny brethren in the church . . . speaking in all sorts of languages." From this it might seem that Irenæus had been a witness to real examples of speaking with tongues. In the other place in which he speaks of the gift (III, 12, 1) he refers to the Day of Pentecost itself, and thus is distinguishing the two gifts; "When the Holy Ghost had descended upon the Disciples, that all should prophesy and speak with tongues." In his day it was evidently most uncommon, for in a detailed treatment of the gifts of the Spirit of which numberless instances happened every day he speaks only of exorcisms of demons, prophetic visions and utterances, healings, and some cases of raising of the dead. In his mention of tongues it was something he had heard of as happening, not something he had known of personally. It is a significant fact also that Justin Martyr (c. 155 A.D.) mentions only prophetic gifts, but no speaking with tongues.

Montanus (c. 156 A.D.) is quoted by Epiphanius as saying in the name of God: "Behold the man is as a lyre and I play over him like a plectron; the man sleeps and I wake; behold it is the Lord who takes away the hearts of men, and gives to me a [another] heart." It was said that Montanus was seized by the Spirit and suddenly placed in a state of rapture and ecstasy. He then began to talk, uttering strange words, and prophesying contrary to the traditional customs of the church. Mithades says this ecstatic state of the pseudo-prophet was begun by a voluntary unconsciousness and continued in an involuntary raising of the soul. The Montanists, however, while characterized by the same ecstatic seizures as those who spoke with tongues must be thought of rather as prophets, for they neither attempted to speak foreign languages nor the unintelligible prattle known in the Corinthian Church.

There is also an obscure passage in Tertullian's (160-220 A.D.) work against Marcion. (Book V, Chap. 8.) It is as follows: "When he mentions the fact that 'it is written in the law,' how that the Creator would speak with other tongues and other lips, whilst confirming indeed the gift of tongues by such a mention, he yet cannot be thought to have affirmed that the gift was that of another god by his reference to the Creator's prediction." Somewhat more exactly he says, "Let Marcion show the gifts of his god! Let [him point out to us] some prophets who speak, not according to human reason but by the Spirit of God, who announce the future and reveal the secrets of the heart! Let him produce a psalm, a vision, a prayer,—I mean a spiritual [prayer pronounced] in ecstasy, that is to say outside of consciousness,—if an interpretation of the tongue is given." Here Tertullian seems to agree

35

with the Pauline account but goes some steps further, giving ecstatic utterances an apologetic value, which Paul never claimed, and insisting on an interpretation which would be reasonable and valuable.

Origen (185-254 A.D.) says of St. Paul, "I suppose that he was made debtor to different nations, because, through the grace of the Holy Spirit, he had received the gift of speaking in the languages of all nations; as he himself also saith,—'I speak in tongues more than you all.' Since then any one receives the knowledge of languages, not for himself but for their sake to whom the Gospel is to be preached, he is made debtor to all those of whose language he received the knowledge from God." Origen has also preserved for us an interesting description of speaking in tongues in the ecstatic prophets of his time. He quotes the philosopher Celsus, an earnest opponent of Christendom, who says that many with the appearance of beggars or soothsayers pronounce threatenings of doom of great length, and then add words unintelligible, obscure, and half crazy, the sense of which no reasonable person can understand. The words are not clear, and amount to nothing, but they afford each beggar or impostor an opportunity to use this means of impressing people for his own benefit. This probably refers to speaking with tongues. At the time of Chrysostom (345-407 A.D.) the gift seems to have entirely disappeared, and

36

he is puzzled by Paul's account of the Corinthian situation. He says, "The whole passage is exceedingly obscure; and the obscurity is occasioned by our ignorance of the facts and the cessation of happenings which were common in those days but unexampled in our own."

Subsequent to post apostolic times Paul's value of this gift was not considered the right one, and in the Middle Ages the saints are said to have received the gift and used it for speaking with people of other tongues in their missionary labor. It is rather surprising, however, that in this age of wonders it appeared so infrequently. In fact we find it seldom referred to at all. Görres[1] gives the longest list of any I have noted, and for that reason I quote it, notwithstanding its length. In speaking of the complementary gifts of speaking with and of interpreting tongues he says:

"Sometimes, indeed, the man is heard by others speaking in his own language; and in this case it is not he upon whom the gift reposes but upon those who listen to it. But at other times, to the contrary, he speaks to his auditors in the language which belongs to each of them, and then it is truly he who received the gift of tongues.

"This gift, which the apostles received at the day of Pentecost, we find again later among the hermits

[1] *La Mystique divine, naturelle, et diabolique*, I, pp. 451 ff.

of the desert. Thus it is related of St. Pachomius who, wishing to speak with a brother who knew only the Roman language, of which he himself was ignorant, received the power after having prayed three hours. This gift is reproduced often in modern times, though many times a supernatural gift has been confounded with that which was only the effect of a natural aptitude. Cardinal Mezzofanti, a short time dead, has been the most remarkable man in this way. Again Dominick of Neisse in Silesia, who died in 1650, librarian of the Escorial, can be cited. In addition to most of the languages of Europe he also knew Tartan, Indian, Chaldean, Hebrew, Syriac, Japanese, Chinese, and Persian. But it is impossible to attribute to a natural aptitude that which is told of Ange Clarénus, who received in 1300, during Christmas night, knowledge of the Greek language. It is related in Chapter II of the second book of the Life of St. Dominick that this saint, going from Toulon to Paris and having arrived at Pierre d'Amont, passed the night in prayer in the Notre Dame Church of the place with the brother Bertrand, his travelling companion. The next morning as they went on their way together, they encountered some Germans who were travelling like them. These, seeing them recite their psalms and prayers often, joined themselves to them for prayer with them; and for four days they invited them to partake of their repast, and had all

manner of respect for them. The fourth day, the
saint sighing said to his companion; 'Brother, I truly
reproach myself for receiving temporal gifts from
these strangers, and for not occupying ourselves with
their eternal interests. If you wish it, we will go
kneel down and pray God that he teach us their language, for we are not able to announce to them the
Lord Jesus.' He set himself then to prayers, and
commenced immediately to speak German to the
great astonishment of these strangers; and for four
days more he discoursed with them concerning the
Lord Jesus. When they arrived at Orleans, the Germans, quitting them, commended themselves to their
prayers. The same thing came to the saint at another
time under similar circumstances.

"We have above stated the proofs of this same
gift in St. Vincent Ferrier. St. Antony of Padua,
preaching in Rome to the people who gathered there
from all parts to procure indulgences, all his auditors heard him in their own language, as a great
number later testified. St. Francis Xavier spoke the
languages of people to whom he announced the Gospel as easily as if he was born among them. Often
when he preached at the same time to men of different nations, each understood in his language that
which caused veneration for him, and gave a singular authority to his work. The same thing is told of
St. Louis Bertrand and of Martin Valentine. Jean of

St. Francis also obtained from God in prayer the knowledge of the Mexican tongue, and immediately set himself to preaching in this language, to the great astonishment of all hearers. This gift was also accorded to St. Stephen in his missions in Georgia; so that he spoke Greek, Turkish, and Armenian so fluently that natives held him in admiration. It is also said of St. Colette that she had the gift of tongues; and among those which she learned in this manner Latin and German are cited. The Abbe Trithème reports the same thing of the Abbess Elizabeth. A French woman named Marguerite came one day to see St. Claire of Monte Falcone, who spoke French with her a long time, although she had never learned this language. The blessed Jeanne of the Cross had this gift when she was in ecstasy; and she was able to communicate in different languages, according to the needs of her auditors, the light which she received from on High. Two Mohammedans who could not decide to embrace Christianity were brought to her one day. She had an ecstasy, and spoke Arabic with them; so that they finished by demanding baptism. Jeanne instructed them later in her ecstasy of the truths of the faith."

Various accounts are given by different writers concerning the experiences of certain saints with the gift of tongues. In interpreting these we shall have to remember the tendency of legends to increase in their miraculous features, the further they are removed in time from the writer.

The gift which St. Pachomius (292-348 A.D.) is said to have enjoyed was confined to the use of the Greek and Latin languages which he sometimes miraculously spoke, and which he never learned. This was given to him at times after special prayer for the power to meet some immediate need.[1]

St. Hildegard (1098-1179 A.D.), although she was uneducated, after a strange experience—a fiery light went through her brain, breast, and heart which was like a flame not burning but warming—could understand and interpret the Holy Scriptures without having a grammatical knowledge of the Latin language. She also had an entirely unknown language, the writings of which are still preserved in Weisbaden. She not only spoke and wrote in this strange language, but she also made a German translation. Of this Baring-Gould says: "She also pretended to speak in an unknown tongue, and to be able to interpret this language. The study of this pretended new language is suggestive and amusing. It has been taken in hand by Grimm, Pitra, and Roth. It presents an amusing jumble of words, German, Latin, and misunderstood Hebrew."[2]

[1] A. Butler, *Lives of the Saints*, May 14; J. J. Görres, *op. cit.*, p. 451.

[2] Baring-Gould, *Virgin Saints and Martyrs*, p. 294.

St. Vincent Ferrier (1357-1419 A.D.) is credited
with the gift of tongues, although the miracle seems
to have been similar to that of Pentecost, in the ears
of the hearers rather than in the tongues of the
speakers. It is said of him by one authority: "While
he always spoke the dialect of Valentia, his native
place, all understood him as if he had spoken to each
in his own dialect. At Genoa he had for auditors
Greeks, Germans, Sardes, Hungarians, and others
who understood only their mother tongue, and who,
nevertheless, at the end of the sermon affirmed that
they had not lost a single word of it." Others say
that he preached in Latin and his native dialect, and
Baillet affirmed that he preached in French, Spanish,
and Italian, and, where these languages were not
understood, in Latin, apparently seeing nothing miraculous in the saint's speaking different languages.
Not only did others comprehend him when he spoke,
but it is said that he comprehended the Bretons who
knew no language but their own.[1]

Butler's reference to St. Francis Xavier (1506-
1552 A.D.), as far as the gift of tongues is concerned,
is as follows: "When the holy man first penetrated
into the inland provinces of the Indians, being
wholly ignorant of the language of the people, he

[1] A. Butler, *Lives of the Saints*, April 5; J. J. Görres, *La
Mystique divine, naturelle, et diabolique*, I, p. 443; P. Schaff,
History of the Apostolic Church, p. 198.

could only baptize children and serve the sick, who
by signs could signify what they wanted, as he wrote
to F. Mansilla. Whilst he exercised his zeal in Trav-
ancore, God first communicated to him the gift of
tongues, according to the relation of a young Portu-
guese of Coimbra, named Vaz, who attended him in
many of his journeys. He spoke very well the language of those barbarians without having learned it,
and had no need of an interpreter when he instructed
them. . . . The gift of tongues was a transient
favor. . . . At Amanguchi, God restored to St.
Francis the gift of tongues; for he preached often to
the Chinese merchants, who traded there, in their
mother-tongue, which he had never learned."

White chooses the experience of St. Francis, however, in connection with the speaking with tongues,
as an example of the growth of a legend without any
basis of fact in life experience. He says:

"Throughout his letters, from first to last, Xavier
constantly dwells upon his difficulties with the various languages of the different tribes among whom he
went. He tells us how he surmounted these difficulties: sometimes by learning just enough of a language to translate into it some of the main Church
formulas; sometimes by getting the help of others
to patch together some pious teachings to be learned
by rote; sometimes by employing interpreters; and
sometimes by a mixture of various dialects, and even

43

by signs. On one occasion he tells us that a very serious difficulty arose, and that his voyage to China was delayed because, among other things, the interpreter he had engaged had failed to meet him.

"In various *Lives* which appeared between the time of his death and his canonization this difficulty is much dwelt upon; but during the canonization proceedings at Rome, in the speeches then made, and finally in the papal bull, great stress was laid upon the fact that Xavier possessed *the gift of tongues*. It was declared that he spoke to the various tribes with ease in their languages. This legend of Xavier's miraculous gift of tongues was especially mentioned in the papal bull, and was solemnly given forth by the pontiff as an infallible statement to be believed by the universal Church. Gregory XV having been prevented by death from issuing the *Bull of Canonization,* it was finally issued by Urban VIII; and there is much food for reflection in the fact that the same Pope who punished Galileo, and was determined that the Inquisition should not allow the world to believe that the earth revolves about the sun, thus solemnly ordered the world, under pain of damnation, to believe in Xavier's miracles, including his 'gift of tongues,' and the return of the crucifix by the pious crab. But the legend was developed still further: Father Bouhours tells us, 'The holy man

spoke very well the language of those barbarians
without having learned it, and had no need of an
interpreter when he instructed.' And, finally, in our
own time, the Rev. Father Coleridge, speaking of the
saint among the natives says, 'He could speak the
language excellently, though he had never learned it.'

"In the early biography, Tursellinus writes:
'Nothing was a greater impediment to him than his
ignorance of the Japanese tongues; for, ever and
anon, when some uncouth expression offended their
fastidious and delicate ears, the awkward speech of
Francis was a cause of laughter.' But Father Bouhours, a century later, writing of Xavier at the same
period says, 'He preached in the afternoon to the
Japanese in their language, but so naturally and
with so much ease that he could not be taken for a
foreigner.'

"And finally, in 1872, Father Coleridge, of the
Society of Jesus, speaking of Xavier at this time,
says, 'He spoke freely, flowingly, elegantly, as if he
had lived in Japan all his life.'

"Nor was even this sufficient: to make the legend
complete, it was finally declared that, when Xavier
addressed the natives of various tribes, each heard
the sermon in his own language in which he was
born.

"All this, as we have seen, directly contradicts not

only the plain statement of Xavier himself, and various incidental testimonies in the letters of his associates, but the explicit declaration of Father Joseph Acosta. The latter historian dwells especially on the labour which Xavier was obliged to bestow on the study of the Japanese and other languages, and says, 'Even if he had been endowed with the apostolic gift of tongues, he could not have spread more widely the glory of Christ.'

"It is hardly necessary to attribute to the orators and biographers generally a conscious attempt to deceive. The simple fact is, that as a rule they thought, spoke, and wrote in obedience to the natural laws which govern the luxuriant growth of myth and legend in the warm atmosphere of love and devotion which constantly arises about great religious leaders in times when men have little or no knowledge of natural law, when there is little care for scientific evidence and when he who believes most is thought most meritorious."[1]

The gifts of tongues, of prophecy, and of miracles were favors conferred by heaven on a new apostle, St. Louis Bertrand (1526-1581 A.D.), as the authentic history of his life and the bull of his canonization assure us. The bull ascribes to him the gift by

---

[1] A. Butler, *Lives of the Saints*, Dec. 3; A. White, *History of the Warfare of Science with Theology*, II, pp. 19-21; J. J. Görres, *ibid.*, p. 451 ff.; P. Schaff, *op. cit.*, p. 198.

which he is said in three years to have converted 30,000 Indians, of various tribes and dialects, in South America.[1]

[1] A. Butler, *Lives of the Saints*, Oct. 9; J. J. Görres, *ibid.*, I, p. 451; P. Schaff, *op. cit.*, p. 198.

CHAPTER IV

THE LITTLE PROPHETS OF THE CEVENNES

LOUIS XIV, who revoked the Edict of Nantes in 1685, replied to the obstinate refusal of the Huguenots to surrender their religious liberty by beginning to persecute them vigorously. The persecution once started, nothing which the state could do was denied those who conducted and encouraged it. Tens of thousands left their homes for countries where religious toleration was vouchsafed them, but those who were left behind were subjected to every conceivable cruelty, and, according to his own estimate, De Baville, the Intendant of Languedoc, sent ten thousand to the stake, the galleys, or the wheel. Special attention was given to the pastors, who were the natural leaders, and who suffered most. Meetings of Protestants were prohibited, but continued to be held in more and more remote and sheltered places, for the Huguenots considered the preaching service a great means of grace. The sternest measures had little effect, and a passion for martyrdom seemed to spread among the people.

Considering the high emotional state in which the Cevennols were continually kept and the nervous strain caused by the fear of persecution or death, it is not strange that extraordinary phenomena began to appear, and showed themselves by physical manifestations and by prophetic utterances. "In times of great persecution the parts of the Holy Scriptures which foretell coming disasters, which rehearse the tribulations through which the chosen people of God must pass and their ultimate triumph through the signal overthrow of their oppressors, are wont to be favorite subjects of study and contemplation. Thus it was that the book of Daniel in the Old Testament, and the Apocalypse in the New Testament gave color to the thoughts and anticipations of the devout men and women among the Huguenots of the South, who looked for the speedy redemption of their people. What formed the burden of their hopes and desires, they felt themselves compelled of God to utter for the incitement and guidance of their brethren. That many sincerely believed themselves inspired by the Holy Ghost in these deliveries, we can scarcely doubt."[1] In addition to the highly nervous state of "Les enfants de Dieu," as they called themselves, and the inspiration of the descriptions and examples of the Bible, another factor undoubtedly had some casual relation. The meetings held at dead of night, in caves and other weird places, when the darkness and surroundings naturally had a disorganizing tend-

[1] H. M. Baird, "The Camisard Uprising, etc.," *Papers of the American Society of Church History*, vol. II, pt. I, p. 17.

ency, undoubtedly helped to form the special conditions which brought strange phenomena into existence. The sounds from the air, so prominent in the beginning of the manifestations, could not very well have been heard in broad daylight.

"This religious exaltation began in the province of Vivarais, from the time of the *dragonades* and the Revocation [of the Edict of Nantes]. The fourth pastoral letter of Jurieu, dated the 15th of October, 1686, mentions that a man belonging to Cadognav had seen a vision, and heard a voice, which said to him, 'Go, and console my people.' In Béarn and elsewhere, simple people fancied that they had heard the singing of psalms in the air, and had witnessed miraculous apparitions."[1]

Apart from this quotation there seems to be no reference to the man of Cadognav, but all other authorities refer to the sounds in the air as the primary manifestations of these strange occurrences. Thus Heath says: "The first sign of the coming spiritual eruption was that people everywhere began to hear strange sounds in the air; the sound of a trumpet and a harmony of voices. They did not doubt that this music was celestial. It was the note of coming war, the song of the angelic hosts, who, seeing the worship of the poor Cevennols overthrown, offered

[1] G. de Felice, *History of the Protestants of France, etc.*, trans. Barnes, p. 355.

it up on their behalf. So the pious thought and wrote their solemn testimony to their friends in Holland and Switzerland."[1]

Various accounts of what actually was seen and heard in the mountains have been given, all agreeing in the general description. Some lay more emphasis on the musical sounds and others on the spoken words. Without doubt the acoustic variations of the mountainous region, where different meetings were being held at the same time and where sounds in the clear night air were audible for great distances, account for some experiences, but the phenomenon of collective hallucinations, both visual and auditory, exercised in times of great stress, is the more likely explanation.

More wonderful experiences, however, were in store for these stricken people,—experiences which were needed for their encouragement in the unequal contest which they were to wage. Prophets arose in their midst, and the young and untutored spoke words of wisdom and of hope. Finding no help on earth, this celestial language through those who were normally unable either to express such thought or to use such language, was proof to them of the divine origin of the message and of the justice of their cause. The eyes of all Europe were turned toward the

[1] R. Heath, "The Little Prophets of the Cevennes," *Cont. Rev.,* Jan. 1886, p. 121.

Cevennes and the religious fanatics through whom it was said that God was communicating.

Among the first to show this prophetic gift was Isabeau Vincent, the shepherdess of Dauphiny, a young girl who could neither read nor write. She was the daughter of a weaver who had accepted royal gold as the price of his Huguenot faith, and had forced his daughter to attend the Roman Catholic Church. At ten years of age she had been shocked at seeing the dragonades sabre women and children who were worshipping in one of their churches, and not content with that the merciless soldiers had set fire to the building while the congregation was still worshipping and then prevented all exit. She had seen the church burn to the melody of the glory hymns of those perishing Huguenots. She left the home of her father where she had been so badly treated and fled to the home of her godfather. The exact date of her marvellous experience has been preserved; it was February 12, 1688. In this ecstasy she was at first in a sort of stupor, and afterward she became insensible to exterior surroundings, and nothing could arouse her. She stood and spoke, exhorting all to repent, especially those who, like her father, had sold their Lord for money. "For the first five weeks," says Jurieu, "she spoke during her ecstasies no language but that of her country, because her only auditors were the peasantry of the village.

The noise of this miracle having spread, people who understood and spoke French came to see her. She then began to speak French, and with a diction as correct as if she had been brought up in the first houses of Paris. She composed admirable and excellent prayers. Her action had no violence. Her lips moved slightly, and without the least appearance of convulsion."[1] Heath gives us an account of her speech and of her later career in the following words: "What she said was rarely peculiar; she sometimes repeated portions of the mass in Latin, and then refuted what she had recited. Physicians came to see her, but they found her pulse quite normal and every sign of bodily health. She never complained of being tired, even when she had been talking three, or even five, hours during the night, but went to her labor in the ordinary way. She was arrested, and after being led about in different places was confined in a convent. They shaved her head, took away her clothes, lest they were enchanted, and the priests came to exorcise her. According to Debrueys, she was converted to the Catholic faith, and led a pious life, but it must be always remembered that Debrueys was a dramatist by nature."[2]

Smiles[3] says that she would not recant, and so

[1] P. Jurieu, *Lettres Pastorales, etc.,* III, p. 60.

[2] R. Heath, "The Little Prophets of the Cevennes," *Cont. Rev.,* Jan. 1886, p. 122.

[3] S. Smiles, *The Huguenots in France, etc.,* p. 90.

was imprisoned at Greville and afterward in the Tower of Constance. "You may take my life," she said, "but God will raise up others to speak better things than I have done." So it seems to have been.

With this example, which attracted such widespread attention, it was not surprising that many other prophets soon appeared. With the well-known phenomenon of psychic contagion, which manifests itself so frequently among people in the same nervous condition as were the Cevennols, we can easily credit the words of Peyrat[1] that there were in Languedoc no less than a thousand prophets before the end of the first year after the appearance of Isabeau Vincent. The contagion spread from Dauphiny to Viserais, and from there into the Cevennes. "I have seen," said Marshal Villars,[2] "things that I could never have believed if they had not passed un-

[1] N. Peyrat, *Histoire des Pasteurs du Desert.*

[2] *Vie du Marechal de Villars*, I, p. 125. The whole passage, contained in a letter to the Secretary of State, Chamillars, Sept. 25, 1704, is interesting, especially in his unconcerned admission that he murdered in cold blood a poor woman who had an attack in his presence. His words are: "J'ai vu dans ce genre des chose que je n'aurois jamais crues si elles ne s'étoient passies sous mes yeux: une ville entière, dont toutes les femmes et les filles, sans exception, paroissoient possedées du diable. Elles trembloient et prophetisoient publiquement dans les rues. J'en fis arrêter vingt des plus mechantes, dont une eut la hardiesse de trembler et prophetiser une heure devant moi. Je la fis pendre pour l'example, et renfermer les autres dans des hospitaux." For exact text for transcribing see *Papers of the American Society of Church History*, vol. II, pt. I, p. 19.

der my own eyes—an entire city, in which all the women and girls, without exception, appeared possessed by the devil; they quaked and prophesied publicly in the streets." Flottard says there were eight thousand persons in one province who had the inspiration. They were not, however, equally inspired. Heath tells us that between June 1688 and the following February there arose in the Dauphiny, and then in the Vivarais, five or six hundred prophets of both sexes.

As is usual in such cases, the prophetic trance was ushered in with physical manifestations, differing to a certain extent in various districts and among different people. Among these physical manifestations were "a heaving of the chest, a rising of the skin, a more than natural fire in the eyes, and often a fainting fit, and when recovered from the swoon, they spoke with supernatural fluency, sometimes exhorting, at others commanding, and almost always prophesying." These symptoms are not unusual and we have noticed them in connection with certain revivals of a supernatural emotional tone, such as that of the Kentucky revival of 1800. At that time, also, young children preached for hours until entirely exhausted. It was the physical manifestations, however, which seemed to attract attention abroad. The Earl of Shaftesbury tells us that so well known were the Cevennol prophets in 1707 that a puppet-show at Bartholomew Fair represented them with considerable acceptance. He concludes, "There doubtless their strange voices and involuntary agitations are admirably acted, by the emotion of wires, and inspiration of pipes."[1] Benjamin Franklin tells us his first employer, Keimer, the printer of Philadelphia, "had been one of the French Prophets and could act their enthusiastic agitations."[2] Sir Richard Bulkley, a wealthy English baronet, became a convert to the faith of some of the Cevennol refugees who came to London. He declares that he heard John Lacy, one of their leaders, repeat long sentences in Latin, and another refugee speak in Hebrew, neither one of whom could speak a single word in these languages when not in spiritual ecstasy. John Wesley[3] referred to the Cevennol prophets when refuting Dr. Middleton's statement that, after apostolic times, there was not in all history one instance, even so much as mentioned, of any particular person who pretended to exercise this gift. Wesley said: "Sir, your memory fails you again. It has undoubtedly been pretended to, and that at no great distance, either, from our time or country. It has been heard of more than once, no further off than the valleys of Dauphiny.

[1] Anthony, Earl of Shaftesbury, *Letters concerning Enthusiasm to my Lord Summers, Characteristics*, I, 26-28.

[2] *Works of Benjamin Franklin*, ed. J. Bigelow, vol. I, p. 66.

[3] *Wesley's Works*, vol. V, p. 744.

Nor is it yet fifty years ago since the Protestant inhabitants of those valleys so loudly pretended to this and other miraculous powers, as to give much disturbance to Paris itself. And how did the King of France confute this pretense and prevent its being heard any more? Not by the pen of his scholars, but by (a truly heathen way) the swords and bayonets of his dragoons." Hayes[1] very aptly remarks: "We think that it was the sword and bayonet that caused them, rather than caused them to cease. When peace came these supposedly supernatural phenomena were no longer seen."

In addition to these physical manifestations connected with the prophets, other marvels appeared. We are told "when people were obliged to attend prayer meetings at midnight, and found difficulty in tracing the way to the general rendezvous, that some averred a bright star, detached from the heavens, glided before them to give light to their path, and was carried like a lanthorn by the hand of an invisible agent, and on such nights the sound of harps and melodies of ineffable sweetness were heard on the solitary heights, celebrating the coming deliverance of the children of God."[2]

One characteristic which distinguished this phenomenon from other similar experiences was the ex-

[1] D. A. Hayes, *The Gift of Tongues*, p. 70.
[2] A. E. Bray, *The Revolt of the Cevennes, etc.*, p. 66.

treme youth of most of the prophets. It was indeed
rare for an old person to have the spirit of prophecy.
Some of these were children, and some even infants;
one, a baby at the breast, was declared to have
spoken "the wonders of the Lord." Not only at this
time, but at a later outbreak in 1700, when it became very common, it was as much distinguished as
at this time for the youth of its subjects. According
to testimonies made in London in 1707 many children between three and twelve years of age were
among the prophets. "Guillaume Brugiese saw a
little boy, three years old, seized by the spirit, fall
on the ground, strike his breast, saying it was his
mother's sins that thus caused him to suffer; then he
exhorted the bystanders to fight the good fight of
faith, and repent of their sins, for these were the last
times. Jacques du Bois had seen sixty children, between three and twelve, who thus prophesied. Durand Fage heard one night a little girl of eleven
pray and preach a sermon three-quarters of an hour
long, and the words of these young prophets had all
the power that has ever attended analogous movements."[1]

Not only children, but childish men and women
were seized with the ecstasy and prophesied. "Claude
Arnassan relates that a shepherd who was regarded
as incapable of instruction, and who had moreover

[1] R. Heath, *ibid.*, p. 123.

never attended divine worship, being taken to a meeting was on his return seized in the usual way and began to prophesy. A similar case is given by Jacques Mazel, and in a third a woman, considered almost idiotic, uttered discourses of so elevated a character, and in such good French, that her hearers said, 'This ass of Balaam has a mouth of gold.' "

Had there been a more humane man in charge of the persecution, the children might have escaped the fate of their elders, but De Baville was cruel and unflinching. "Without more ado he seized about three hundred of the young prophets, threw them into prison, and sent for the faculty at Montpellier to come and report on their state. The physicians examined the children carefully, found that they were in good health, and clearly not lunatics in the ordinary acceptation of the word. What then was the matter with them! The priests suggested demoniacal possession, but this was a little too much for men of science in the days of Newton and Leibnitz; the faculty reported that the children were fanatics—a very useful word, for it covered their ignorance and sounded alarming enough to justify De Baville in any proceedings he thought fit. The youths were accordingly sent to the galleys, or drafted into the army; the younger children returned to their parents with the caution that if they allowed them to prophesy their homes would be razed to the ground.

Certain prophets peculiarly noted were then put to death."[1]

There were four degrees of ecstasy: the calling or warning, the whisper or inspiration, the prophecy, and the gift or the inspiration in its highest degree. No one can doubt the sincerity of the ecstatics; they obeyed the Spirit, which they said filled them, without reservation, hesitation, or delay, although they were led to certain death. One of their number said of himself, "I always felt in this state an extraordinary elevation to God, before whom I therefore sware that I have neither been dazzled nor misled by any man, nor induced by worldly considerations to utter throughout any other words than those formed by the spirit or angel of God himself, who at this time made use of my organs of speech. To Him alone I surrender during my ecstasy the guidance of my tongue. . . . I know that then a higher and another Power speaks through me."

Their own testimony was that this Spirit made them better people. According to Marion[2] "The persons who had received the inspiration directly abandoned every kind of licentiousness and vanity. Some who had led a debauched life, first became steady and pious, and everyone who frequented their society also became better behaved, and led an exem-

[1] R. Heath, *op. cit.*, pp. 124 f.
[2] Elie Marion, *Theatre Sacre des Cevennes*, p. 80.

plary life. This spirit begot in us a horror of idolatry, a contempt for the world, charity, internal consolation, hope, and an unleavened joy of heart."

The messages were probably in no way extraordinary, and the content could easily be explained by other than miraculous ways. Heath says: "Two things have to be noted—first, that these prophesyings rarely meant more than preaching as their pastors would have done, and occasional intimations of the approach of friends and enemies, or of other dangers which menaced them; second, that the inspiration was not at command, but came in answer to prayer, and always commenced with the words, 'mon enfant.'"

The facts of the renewed and religiously improved life, and of the message which was delivered, are interesting but not uncommon experiences; the most important phases of the gift were the extraordinary fluency of the young and the illiterate, and the speaking in correct French, which was so different from their native patois. The abnormal state, in which all reserve was removed, and during which subconscious action produced appropriate words, would account for the extraordinary fluency of the prophets; and the fact that their exhortations were "fervent, eloquent, correct, well chosen, appropriate, and mostly in good French, which was not the language they ordinarily spoke, but which they knew through their bibles and religious services," requires only for explanation the phenomenon of exalted memory, a not uncommon experience in similar abnormal states, and one which is not infrequently called in to explain one form of speaking with tongues. No words of French or native patois seem to have been used which might not have been recalled if the memory were sufficiently retentive or reproductive. We believe that retention is practically perfect, and reproduction approximately so, under certain abnormal conditions, when a high nervous tension is involved. While we have probably no better example of the exalted memory type of speaking with tongues than the Little Prophets of the Cevennes, we can see nothing in this or in similar cases which cannot be explained by known psychological laws.

The prophecies, together with some extraordinary cruelty, were destined to have sterner results than the comfort and consolation of a few persecuted and despised Protestant peasants. In the spring of 1702, a young man named Durand Fage attended one of the nocturnal assemblies, armed. A prophetess, who was present, pointed to him and said, "My son, that sword which you bear shall destroy the enemies of the truth." She continued to address him in like manner with great energy, until her enthusiasm became contagious, and a hundred voices echoed her exhortation to go forth and do battle with the enemies of God.[1]

At another meeting a Cevennol, named Stephen Forte, who had just escaped from one of De Baville's dungeons, suddenly appeared, and declared that the angel of God had delivered him as he did St. Peter. "Arm, arm!" he cried with fanatical fervor, "God will return to France the true church of a thousand of his people, and by the arms of the faithful." Many prophets took up a like strain, and it spread through the mountains with the rapidity of lightning. As persecution had reappeared with exaggerated violence, it seemed time to draw the sword in self-defence.

For fifteen years, the Abbé du Cheyla, called by Peyrot, "the arch-priest," commissioned to direct the conversion of the Huguenots, had used his office to commit every sort of crime which his tyranny could devise. In 1702 he captured and most cruelly treated a company of Huguenots who were trying to leave the country. On the following Sunday, July 23d, one of the preaching prophets, Pierre Seguire, preached to the assembly on the mountain top near Abbé du Cheyla's home. There he declared that the Lord had ordered him to take up arms to deliver the captives and to exterminate the arch priest of Moloch. Other prophets added their voices to that of

[1] N. Peyrat, *Histoire des Pasteurs du Desert*, I, p. 285.

Seguire, and men were encouraged to strike a blow for freedom. That night Seguire and fifty others met and solemnly swore to liberate their companions and to destroy the arch priest. The following night they descended upon the mansion of Abbé du Cheyla, delivered their friends from the dungeons in the cellar, killed the priest, his household, and garrison, and burned the mansion to the ground. This was the beginning of a revolt, the wonder of which drew the attention of the whole world and can only be likened to the marvellous deeds of the Maccabees fighting for their homeland against the combined armies of Rome.

It is difficult to describe the uprising of the poor peasants of the Cevennes without going into details which would take us too far afield. But since it was begun by the prophesying, some notice must be taken of it. The leader for the first two years was Jean Cavalier, a mere lad and a baker's apprentice; he was ably seconded by Roland and Castanet. The insurgents were called Camisards, and under that name the insurrection is known. The name probably came from camisa—shirt, either because they used a shirt over their armor to recognize each other in their night attacks, or else because, when they made attacks, they are said to have sought clean linen and to have left their own in its place.

At the beginning of 1703 an immense force was

raised to put down the rebellion and to exterminate the insolent Protestants. An army of 60,000 men was put in the field commanded by Montreval, a marshal of France and one of the ablest of French generals. Under him were three lieutenant generals, three major generals, and three brigadier generals. Before the end of the year the Marshal was calling for more troops, and the insurrection was still progressing. Several times after perpetrating most inhuman cruelties the Marshal thought and even reported that the insurrection was ended, only to find within a few days that the enemy was again on the march, and almost without exception the large force of royal troops failed to conquer the small band of Camisards. In one battle, with a far inferior force, Cavalier captured a large amount of booty and killed a colonel, a major, thirty-three captains or lieutenants, and four hundred and fifty men, while his own loss was only about twenty killed or wounded.

The success of the Camisards was due to their rapid movement, a knowledge of the country, the sympathy of the people, and above all the belief that they were fighting the battle of the Lord. Frequently the tide of battle was turned by the invincible zeal and courage, even to recklessness, with which the Camisards charged. Their battle hymn, Psalm 68, struck terror to their enemies. All were permeated with a religious inspiration. "The Camisard chiefs

were designated by the spirit. They believed themselves to be filled with it, and this was the source of
their courage, their triumphs, and their constancy in
the greatest extremities. Whether the necessity of
the moment was to collect their scattered bands, to
fix the point of attack, to choose the day of combat,
to retreat, to advance, to discover traitors and spies,
to spare prisoners, or to put them to death, it was
the spirit they consulted: everywhere and in all
things their persuasion was that they acted under
the immediate and sovereign direction of heaven."[1]

In 1704 Marshal Montreval was recalled and
Marshal Villars was sent to do what Montreval had
been unsuccessful in accomplishing. He attempted
to do by diplomacy what force of arms had not been
able to accomplish and asked for a conference with
Cavalier. It was agreed to permit liberty of con-
science and worship, release of all prisoners within
six weeks, return of estates and privileges to all
exiles, and no taxes to be paid by the Cevennols
whose homes had been burned. This seems to have
been a real victory for the Protestants, especially
since the Roman Catholics objected strenuously to
the terms. When Cavalier returned to his own leaders and troops, they repudiated him for having made
these terms and continued the insurrection for five
years longer, but with much less force.

[1] G. de Felice, *History of the Protestants in France, etc.*, trans.
Barnes, p. 356.

CHAPTER V

VARIOUS SECTS

THE history of the Christian Church contains accounts of many other, although less important, manifestations of speaking in tongues. It was found among the Jansenists in France in 1731. Miracles were said to have been performed at the tomb of the archdeacon of Paris, who had defended the doctrines of Jansenius. Some people while visiting that tomb experienced ecstasy and convulsive movements that became contagious, and many who were thus seized prophesied and uttered unintelligible expressions in an unconscious state. They often used absolutely senseless combinations of sounds, which passed for words from foreign languages. They believed, as did the Camisards, that their organs of speech were controlled by a superior power. Sometimes they retained full consciousness and remembered all the details when the paroxysms were over, but at other times there was total amnesia. Similarly there were the "calling voices" or the "preaching desire" or the "sermon sickness" of Norway and Sweden in 1841-43. This experience originated in a Christian revival. The phenomenon was mostly found with the young people, sometimes in children from four to twelve years of age. It came suddenly and was irresistible; even praying against its coming, and the closing of the mouth with the hand did not prevent its appearance. Inarticulate sounds alternated with unconscious singing of hymns, and afterward there was rarely any recollection of what had been said.

References are sometimes made to speaking with tongues among the Quakers in the time of Cromwell, but the Quakers themselves apparently made no claims to the possession of this spiritual gift, although they did claim the gift of prophecy. There was undoubtedly extravagance of speech at times, as there was extravagance of action; among devotees who would march through cities naked, and exhume bodies with the expectation of restoring them to life, speaking with tongues would be a minor exhibition, and might well be expected. There were certain portions of their doctrine which might naturally lead to speaking with tongues, and which might cause one to prognosticate some such automatism. The doctrine of the inner light, according to which each one was led and directed personally without regard to others, removed restrictions which naturally curbed the more extravagant. The scorn of human learning, the direct reliance upon inspiration, the tendency to prophesy, and the propagation of their beliefs by speaking rather than by writing also tended to glossolalic expression. The preaching of youth and children and the automatic movements from which they received their name, both favored the outburst of spontaneous speech; but strange to say there was little of it. It may be that the impulse to motor automatisms entirely expressed itself in "quaking" and similar movements.

A sect prone to extravagant speech furnished not a few recruits to the early Quakers; its members were appropriately named Ranters, and were common in the North Midlands of England. They seem, however, to have brought little of their characteristic actions with them into the Society of Friends. Probably nothing shows so clearly the good common sense of George Fox and the other early leaders as the lack of glossolalic expression. Says Braithwaite:[1] "The Quakers, like the first Apostles, seemed to their contemporaries to be filled with new wine, men who turned the world upside down, and it must be admitted that the exuberance of their experiences again and again betrayed them into excesses of conduct and errors of judgment. The Inward Light which possessed them shone through the medium of minds fallible and often ignorant, and was necessarily coloured with many of the fixed ideas which belonged to the Puritanism of the day."

As we look through the histories of Methodism we do not find much of fact concerning the Metho-

[1] W. C. Braithwaite, *The Beginnings of Quakerism*, p. 514.

dist possession of the gift of tongues. There seem, however, to have been many cases in the North of England and in Wales of repeating the same word over and over a great many times during the process or experience of conversion. In *Stevens' History*[1] we find the story of what occurred under the preaching of the Reverend John Berridge of Everton. "The assembly was often swayed with irrepressible emotion, sometimes crying out with groans and sobs, at others pervaded by a sound of loud breathing, like that of people gasping for breath." There seemed also to have been much shouting and uttering of unintelligible sounds. Later we read,[2] "The marvels under the ministration of Berridge at Everton, he [Wesley] believed were at first wholly from God." But whether these phenomena could be called speaking with tongues or much more than a babble is very doubtful. Phenomena of this kind have been more common among the Primitive Methodists than among those of the regular order.

In Mormonism, or the belief of the Latter Day Saints, we find much of the so-called "Gift of Tongues," with which was very closely linked the "Gift of Interpretation." In a summary of Mormon doctrine given by Joseph Smith in 1842 is the following: "Art. 7. We believe in the gifts of tongues,

[1] I, p. 383.
[2] A. Stevens, *The History of Methodism*, II, p. 424.

prophecy, revelation, visions, healing, interpretation of tongues, etc." When a convert to the Mormon belief received to himself the Holy Ghost, he was supposed to receive all the "gifts" of the church, including prophecy, healing, miracle, speaking in tongues, and the interpretation of tongues.[1] However, the gift of tongues and the gift of interpretation are spoken of as being among the minor spiritual phenomena.

These gifts were not prominent from the beginning of Mormonism, but after Joseph Smith had claimed power after power, which he purported to have received direct from heaven, and these revelations were accepted by the people, he brought forth in January 1833, the "Gift of Tongues." This allowed the ignorant and illiterate to utter any jargon or nonsense with the belief that it was a spiritual manifestation. He had a unique way of displaying this power. It would be advertised that at a certain meeting someone would speak with tongues. When that meeting was well under way, Father Smith or Father Rigdon would call upon some illiterate brother to rise and speak in tongues in the name of Jesus Christ. The order given was: "Arise upon your feet, speak or make some sound, continue to make sounds of some kind, and the Lord will make a tongue or language of it." Then after the jargon

[1] J. H. Beadle, *Mysteries and Crimes of Mormonism*, pp. 321, 323.

would cease, some other brother would arise and professedly interpret what was said, in reality repeating the first religious thought that came into his mind.[1] When Sister Bybee spoke in tongues, President Young declared it to be real, and asked what the nations would say if they were there. He said that if he did not restrain the brethren and sisters the Day of Pentecost would be insignificant compared with Mormon manifestations.

Gunnison[2] says of speaking with tongues among these people: "This is not the ancient gift, whereby one, addressing a people speaking a different language from himself, was enabled to talk in their own words. It is, that persons among themselves, in their enthusiastic meetings, shall be 'moved by the spirit' to utter any set of sounds in imitation of words, and, it may be, words belonging to some Indian or other language. The speaker is to know nothing of the ideas expressed, but another, with the 'gift of interpretation of tongues,' can explain to the astonished audience all that has been said. Any sounds, of course then, are a language known to the Lord."

Kennedy gives an account of one apostate of the church, and how he lost his faith. This man, who was a trader, was well acquainted with the Choctaw

[1] J. H. Kennedy, *Early Days of Mormonism,* p. 111.
[2] J. W. Gunnison, *The Mormons or Latter Day Saints, etc.,* p. 53.

Indian language. In one meeting he arose and delivered a long address in that language, and was followed by a brother Mormon who translated this speech in tongues as an account of the glories of the temple, then being constructed, which translation was entirely foreign to the substance of the address.

Gunnison refers to another amusing incident of the gift of tongues, or rather, of the gift of interpretation among the Mormons. He relates the story of a boy who had become so famous in the interpretation of these strange addresses that he was called upon by the elders whenever any difficult case came up. On one occasion when a woman arose suddenly in the meeting and called out, "O mela, meli, melee," the lad was requested to reduce this exclamation to English. He promptly gave the translation, "Oh my leg! my thigh! my knee!" Even when the angry and disgusted elders had him before the council, he persisted that he had given the correct translation. As the woman herself did not know what it meant, they were compelled to give him an admonition and let him go.

Mr. Hawthornthwaite, in giving an account of a meeting at Manchester, when the jargon was used by the Mormons, says: "Those who speak in tongues are generally the most illiterate among the Saints, such as cannot command words as quick as they would wish, and instead of waiting for a suitable word to come to their memories, they break forth in the first sound their tongues can articulate no matter what it is. Thus, some person in the meeting has told an interesting story about Zion, then an excitable brother gets up to bear his 'testimony,' the speed of speech increases with the interest of the subject: 'Beloved brethren and sisters, I rejoice and my heart is glad to overflowing,—I hope to go to Zion, and to see you all there, and to—to—O, me sontro von te, sontro von terre, sontro conte. O me palassate te' and so on.'[1]

Miss Eliza Snow, the Mormon poetess, is reported to have been proficient in this speaking in tongues. She is recorded as being in the habit of rushing into the dwelling of some woman, saying, "Sister, I want to bless you!" and, laying her hands on the other's head, she would utter a blessing in this confused jargon.[2]

Hawthornthwaite[3] says: "At a meeting in Manchester an elder shuts his eyes and at the top of his voice exclaims: 'O me, sontra von te, par las a te se, ter mon te roy ke; ran passan par du mon te! O me, sontrote krush krammon palassate Mount Zion kron cow che and America pa palassate pa pau pu pe!

[1] S. Hawthornthwaite, *Adventures among the Mormons,* pp. 88-91.

[2] J. H. Beadle, *Mysteries and Crimes of Mormonism.*

[3] S. Hawthornthwaite, *Adventures, etc.,* p. 89.

Sontro von teli terattate taw!!!' This was interpreted as follows: 'Yea, beloved sister, thus saith the Lord unto thee, be thou humble and obedient to the priesthood that is placed over thee, and thou shalt be gathered unto the land of Zion, and see the temple of the Lord; yea, thou shalt have thy washings and thine anointings, and thou shalt receive thy blessings! Yea, beloved sister, be thou faithful and obedient, and thou shalt have the desire of thine heart; yea, beloved sister, thou shalt be a mother in Israel, and thou shalt be great, yea, if thou art only humble and faithful, thou shalt be a savior on Mount Zion, and receive thy exaltation in the kingdom of God! Be humble and obedient, dear sister, and these are thy blessings in the name of Jesus Christ.' "

As a further example of the Mormon effort at speaking with tongues, the same author gives this: "O, me, terrei te te-te-te! O, me, terrei te! Terrei, terrei, te, te-te-te! O, me, terrei te!" The alliteration is very noticeable here, as it is in most cases of speaking with tongues. There is a psychological reason for this, which will be pointed out later. Among the Mormons the interpretation of tongues seems to have been a more or less haphazard affair. One example is given of a girl in one of the meetings who spoke only her native Welsh. An elder acquainted with both Welsh and English commonly interpreted for her. Being slow in beginning his interpretation,

75

a strange elder arose and gave an interpretation of what he supposed to be genuine speaking with tongues, and brought disrepute upon himself and his cause by presenting an interpretation entirely different from a translation of the Welsh.

At the dedication of the temple, as one of the number relates, "hundreds of Elders spoke in tongues, but many of them being young in the Church, and never having witnessed the manifestation of this gift before, felt a little alarmed." However, all the elders, who went into countries where other languages were spoken, learned, either before they went or after they got there, that the gift of tongues was not of practical value. While this gift still remains firmly established in the Mormon faith as a spiritual phenomenon, the church has discouraged it because it has brought ridicule and disrespect from the ungodly. As a consequence it is heard far less frequently than formerly. Among this sect it seems never to have been considered a foreign language, which might have been translated by some polyglot attendant of the meeting, but rather a celestial language which had to be interpreted by a saint specially inspired for that purpose.

Among the Shakers, speaking with tongues appears to have been prominent, although at times it is difficult to differentiate it from some other gifts. "Mother" Ann Lee, the founder of this sect, was said to have been proficient in the exercise of this gift. While still in England, she was accused of blasphemy when claiming to speak with tongues, and after her arrest was brought before four clergymen of the Church of England, all noted linguists, for examination. She was there given an opportunity to prove the genuineness of her inspiration. Although she was unable to read or write, according to the records of her followers, the power of God fell upon her and the gift of tongues was imparted to her. She then discoursed to these clergymen, as they testified, in seventy-two different languages, speaking many of them better than they had heard them spoken before. After the examination they advised her persecutors to let her alone.

In addition to the founder, the gift seems to have been imparted to certain of the leaders and preachers of the order, such as Father William (a brother of Ann), Samuel Johnson, and Richard Bushnell. It is said of Father William that, when a number of Indians visited the colony, he, although entirely ignorant of their language, was enabled to address them in their own tongue, so that they understood him fully. Richard Bushnell, known as Elder Richard, was famed in his day for his fluency in this gift. In more recent times, Eldress Antoinette Doolittle was endowed with this power in a marked degree, although her speech was in an unknown, not a recognizable, foreign tongue. After speaking in this tongue, unknown to herself or her auditors, she was sometimes given the power to interpret the message.

Seth Y. Wells, who became a prominent member of the order, owed his conversion to the impression made on him by the exercise of this gift by members of the colony. When principal of Hudson Academy, he visited an uncle living in one of the Shaker families at Watervliet, N. Y. While attending one of the services, he heard one sister talk in an unknown tongue, and, recognizing the language (we are not told what language it was), he inquired if anyone else knew of what the woman was speaking. "Yea," replied another sister, "she is talking of that journey you are expecting to take." As neither of the sisters knew the language, and as no one was aware of his anticipated journey, he believed in the miraculous character of the experience, and yielded obedience to the divine power which he believed to exist in the Shaker order.

Dancing, so common a religious expression with the sect, and the so-called gift of song were usually and sometimes inextricably mixed with the gift of tongues. Sometimes one of these and not infrequently both were concurrent phenomena. The songs were supposed to be original and the result of inspiration. These furnished fertile conditions for speaking with tongues, for originality has its limits, and the force of inspiration might easily cause utterances without any meaning behind them. We have accounts by eye-witnesses of meetings which began with stamping by all the brothers and sisters. When this abated somewhat, some of the sisters began to speak in unknown tongues. Following this, all the persons in the room started shaking, jumping, turning, and talking in unknown tongues, each contributing to a scene of awful riot and confusion.

One observer[1] sums up his conclusions concerning this gift among the members of this sect as follows: "This gift finds the most patronage among the sisters, and those brethren who are distinguished for their garrulity. While a general display of the characters of the members meets the eye by their performances, we hear the sisters chant their unknown notes in a quick and nasal pronunciation, indicative of their natural effeminacy and loquacity. . . . The weakness of their minds, the volume of their feelings, and their inability to contain them, force this manner of expression; and we are not to wonder when they cannot express themselves clearly, as chaos in thought will be chaos in expression."

The songs in unknown tongues were not dependent upon spontaneous inspiration, but were produced upon the command of the leaders. Especially in their mountain meetings, the elders spoke to the sisters

---

[1] W. J. Haskett, *Shakerism Unmasked,* pp. 194 ff.

and brothers as follows: "The ministry tells us there is a gift of song for us brethren and sisters, now let us every one labor for a song. We must go forth in the gift, brethren and sisters, if we would receive a blessing." Then it is recorded that they would go out under that impression and labor for days and weeks until they broke into such songs in unknown tongues.

The following are two specimens of these songs, the first in a wholly unknown and unknowable tongue:

O calivin Christe I no vole,
Calivin Christe liste um,
I no vole vinin ne viste,
I no vole virte vum.

The second is partly English:

Selera vane van vo canera van re lava,
Dilera van se lane cinera van so vo,
'Tis Mother's holy love, love she sent it by her
   dove, dove, dove,

'Twas vene van se vane, 'twill ever more endure.[1]
Nothing more than a perusal of these songs is needed to disclose their worthlessness. A report of a select committee on the subject of the Shakers, given to the Assembly of the State of New York, April 2, 1849, contains these words: "after a profound silence for some five minutes, they commence singing

[1] D. R. Lamson, *Shakerism as it is*, p. 80.

hymns, the words of which are unintelligible to the auditors."

Another form of speaking with tongues was seen among the Shakers, which was connected with a spiritualistic belief. At certain times the spirits of departed people, perhaps of some Indians, would seem to enter the members, and to act and speak through them. Thus it might happen that during a meeting a sister would be seen to jump up and dance and sing, supposedly expressing the dancing and singing of some departed Indian chief. One sister, Sister Sally, being persuaded by the elders and inspired by the drinking of native spirits, danced to the tune and words of the following nonsensical doggerel:

> Te he, te haw, te hoot, te te hoot,
> Me be mother's pretty pappoose,
> Me ting, me dant, te I diddle um,
> Because me here to whites come,
> He di diddy, ti diddle O;
> Round, around, and round me go,
> Me leap, me jump, e up and down,
> On good whitey, shiny ground.[1]

It may seem strange, from a religious standpoint, to ascribe to any but the Holy Spirit the power to inspire the gift of tongues, for, whatever else the

[1] D. R. Lamson, *op. cit.*, p. 68.

New Testament may teach concerning the matter, it is never hinted that this gift may come from any other source, least of all from a demoniacal one. It is to be noted, however, that the Roman ritual puts among the number of signs of demoniacal possession the power of speaking or understanding a tongue which one does not know, and the church has always admitted the existence of diabolical counterfeits of divine gifts. Today demoniacal possession is hardly an accredited religious phenomenon, but different forms of insanity or degeneracy take its place in our thinking and vocabulary. However we may designate the infirmity, we find in the history of the church a number of cases in which speaking with tongues was one of the symptoms. A few reported cases will be given in the following paragraphs.

In an orphanage in Amsterdam, in 1566, seventy children were seized with what was supposed to have been demoniacal possession. They climbed on walls and roofs like cats, and made horrible faces when anyone approached them. They could talk in foreign languages which they had never learned, and related events which happened at the same moment in other places.

Soon after the middle of the nineteenth century demoniacal possession manifested itself in the little village of Morzin in Haute-Savoie. A little girl with some sort of convulsion was cured by means of a relic, and the demon was thus supposed to have been exorcised. Later, other girls were similarly afflicted. During the attacks it is said that they uttered terrible blasphemies, experienced hallucinations, revealed secrets, prophesied, and spoke Latin, German, and Arabic, languages which they had never learned.

Peebles[1] relates an incident told him by a cultured Brahmin in India. The son of this Brahmin, a boy of fifteen, suffered from strange spells which increased in frequency. During these seizures he seemed normal except somewhat more sensitive, nervous, and suspicious, and he would speak in a strange voice or in different voices, and when using one voice his speech was a wild gibberish. The temple priest assured the father that his son was obsessed. The same author gives the case of a woman supposed to be possessed by the spirit of an outcast Indian squaw, during which time she talked gibberish intermixed with some profane words.

Nevius[2] quotes the translation of an extract from a communication of Wang Yung-ngen of Peking. After referring to a case of possession which he had known, he said: "I have known many other cases which it is unnecessary to record in full. It may be said in general of possessed persons, that sometimes

[1] J. M. Peebles, *The Demonism of the Ages and Spirit Obsession*, p. 105.

[2] J. L. Nevius, *Demon Possession and Allied Themes*, p. 58.

people who cannot sing, are able when possessed to do so; others who ordinarily cannot write verses, when possessed compose in rhyme with ease. Northern men will speak languages of the south, and those of the east the language of the west; and when they awake to consciousness they are utterly oblivious of what they have done."

The same author quotes from the biography of Reverend John Christopher Blumhardt, who died in 1880, and who became famous for his prayer cures. Perhaps his most noted cure was that in Möttlengen, Germany, of Gottliebin Dittus, who was believed to be possessed by demons. While dealing with this case, "Blumhardt held conversations with several of the demons, one of whom proclaimed himself a perjurer, and yelled again and again: 'Oh, man, think of eternity. Waste not the time of mercy; for the day of judgment is at hand.' These demons spoke in all the different European languages, and in some which Blumhardt and others present did not recognize."

Görres,[1] after quoting other cases, says: "Doctor Th. Bartholini relates, following Hannemann, . . . that in the year 1673 a young soldier of eighteen years found himself possessed. Two years before, he had given himself to a demon for four years. His language was unintelligible; but by intervals he

[1] *La Mystique divine, naturelle, et diabolique*, IV, p. 473.

knew how to express himself in a clear and precise manner, and then he was able to respond to each in his language, whether in French, or in Latin or otherwise. In his paroxysms, four very strong men were hardly able to hold him. Cameralius tells that a demon, who possessed a woman, when he wished to speak Greek, made the savants who were present laugh on account of his poor pronunciation. He excused himself by saying that he knew very well that he had a bad accent, but that the fault of it was in the woman whose tongue was not able to adapt itself to pronounce strange words."

Hammond[1] gives us an account of a girl who, previous to a cataleptic seizure, while in a state of ecstasy, would talk in a foreign tongue. He says, "A young girl, recently under my professional care, was cataleptic on an average once a week, and epileptic twice or three times in the intervals. Five years previously she had spent six months in France, but had not acquired more than a very slight knowledge of the language, scarcely, in fact, sufficient to enable her to ask for what she wanted at her meals. Immediately before her cataleptic seizure she went into a state of ecstasy, during which she recited poetry in French, and delivered harangues about virtue and godliness in the same language. She pronounced at

[1] W. A. Hammond, *Spiritualism and Nervous Derangement*, p. 292.

these times exceedingly well, and seemed never at a loss for a word. To all surrounding influences she was apparently dead. But she sat bolt upright in her chair, her eyes staring at vacancy, and her organs of speech in constant action. Gradually she passed into the cataleptic paroxysm. She was an excellent example of what Mrs. Hardinge calls a 'trance medium.' The materialistic influence of bromide of potassium, however, cured her catalepsy and epilepsy, destroyed her knowledge of the French tongue and made her corporeal structure so gross that the spirits refused to make further use of it for their manifestations."

The cases gathered together here may seem to be unrelated and heterogeneous, but psychologically they are very similar. The foundation of all is the abnormal state of trance or ecstasy in which certain mental powers are exalted, chief among which are the memory and the power of expression. At the same time the higher judicial and regulative mental functions are almost entirely inhibited. While in this state, the suggestion of being another person has all the effect of such a suggestion during the hypnotic state. The glossolalics endeavor to carry out the part and that without the confusion of bashfulness which would come were the person in a normal state.

CHAPTER VI

EDWARD IRVING AND THE CATHOLIC APOSTOLIC CHURCH

EDWARD IRVING, whose name was most closely identified with the Catholic Apostolic Church, was born at Annan, Dumfriesshire, Scotland, in 1792. While Irvingism was on everyone's tongue between the years 1831-34, and in the third decade of the last century the name of Irving seemed likely to rank among the immortals, the mention of his name carries with it little intelligence to-day. He studied at the University of Edinburgh, and, after completing his course for the ministry, he taught school at Haddington and later at Kirkaldy. A pupil of his at the former place was Jane Welch; when at the latter place, he began his friendship for her future husband, Thomas Carlyle. After acting as assistant to Thomas Chalmers in Glasgow, he accepted the call of the Caledonian Church, Hatton Garden, London, and in a brief time transformed a poor and obscure congregation into a prosperous and fashionable one, giving up the humble chapel for a beautiful building in Regent Square. This was accomplished by the sheer force of his personality and his attractiveness as a preacher. It might be well at this point to get a view of him from his intimate friend, Thomas Carlyle. Of him Carlyle says:

(Letter to John Carlyle, August 21, 1830.)

"Make my kindest compliments to my old friend your landlord (Irving), whose like, take him for all in all, I have not yet looked upon. Tell him that none more honestly desires his welfare; oh were I but joined to such a man! Would the Scotch Kirk but expel him, and his own better genius lead him far away from all Apocalypses, and prophetic and theologic chimeras, utterly unworthy of such a head, to see the world as it here lies visible, and is, that we might fight together for God's true cause even to the death! With one such man I feel as if I could defy the earth."[1]

So much for Carlyle's estimate of the man. His enthusiastic and eccentric characteristics, prior to the supposed outpouring of the Spirit in the gift of tongues may be judged by Carlyle's description in the following letter.

(Letter to John Carlyle, June 10, 1828.)

"We left Edward Irving there preaching like a Boanerges, with (as Henry Inglis very naïvely remarked) the town divided about him, 'one party thinking that he was quite mad, another that he was

[1] J. A. Froude, *Carlyle's Life in London*, II, p. 124.

an entire humbug.' For my own share, I would not
be intolerant of any so worthy a man; but I cannot
help thinking that, if Irving is on the road to truth,
it is no straight one. We had a visit from him, and
positively there does seem a touch of extreme exaltation in him. I do not think he will go altogether mad,
yet what else he will do I cannot so well conjecture.
Cant and enthusiasm are strangely commingled in
him. He preaches in steamboats and all open places,
wears clothes of an antique cut (his waistcoat has
flaps or tails midway down the thigh), and in place
of ordinary salutation bids 'the Lord bless you.' "[1]

Carlyle's father has this characteristic comment,
"What think'st he means gawn up and down the
country tevelling and screeching like a wild boar?"

Irving was a born mystic and a lovable soul. His
writings were mostly upon apocalyptical and mystical subjects, and the great desire of his heart was to
see the church become more spiritual. In 1830 he
was deeply engaged with these thoughts, and was
deploring the coldness of the church, when news
came to him of a marvellous outpouring of the Spirit
in the West of Scotland; this must be the manifestation for which he had longed and prayed, and he was
prepared to receive it.

At Farnicarry there lived an invalid named Mary

[1] Froude, *op. cit.*, II, p. 29.

Campbell. On her sick bed she had meditated on the deplorable condition of the church and especially upon the loss of spiritual gifts in later years. Particularly was she concerned with the lost gift of tongues. A revival was stirring the neighborhood when she astonished all her friends by suddenly speaking in an unknown tongue. We have an account of this strange event from the pen of Irving himself. It is as follows: "The handmaiden of the Lord, of whom He made choice on that night (a Sunday evening in end of March), to manifest forth in her His glory, had been long afflicted with a disease which the medical men pronounced to be a decline, and that it would soon bring her to the grave, whither her sister had been hurried by the same malady some months before. Yet while all around her were anticipating her dissolution, she was in the strength of faith meditating missionary labours among the heathen; and this night she was to receive the preparation of the Spirit; the preparation of the body she received not till some days after. It was on the Lord's day; and one of her sisters, along with a female friend, who had come to the house for the end, had been spending the whole day in humiliation, and fasting, and prayer before God, with a special respect to the restoration of the gifts. They had come up in the evening to the sick-chamber of their sister, who was laid on a sofa, and along with one or two others of the household, they were engaged in prayer together. When, in the midst of their devotion, the Holy Ghost came with mighty power upon the sick woman as she lay in her weakness, and constrained her to speak at great length, and with superhuman strength, in an unknown tongue, to the astonishment of all who heard, and to her own great edification and enjoyment in God,—'for he that speaketh in a tongue edifieth himself.' She has told me that this first seizure of the Spirit was the strongest she ever had; and that it was in some degree necessary it should have been so, otherwise she would not have dared to give way to it."[1] Not long after this a similar experience came to James McDonald of Port Glasgow, who, learning of Mary Campbell's illness, wrote her, commanding her in the name of the Lord Jesus to arise from her sick bed. Immediately on receiving the letter she arose and from that time had good health.

Irving received these phenomena at their face value, and endeavored to have them duplicated in his London church. Accordingly incessant prayer was held, Irving having no eyes to see the overpowering force of suggestion with which such prayers might operate upon sensitive and excitable minds. In July 1831 the wonder appeared, but it was not until four months later that it manifested itself publicly. They

[1] Mrs. Oliphant, *The Life of Edward Irving*, p. 379.

had asked their Master for the wonders of this grace, and when it appeared could they doubt its genuineness? When they asked for bread would He give them a stone? In his great apologetic address before the Presbytery of London, in March 1832, Irving said: "Just as it was with Paul, so with these persons, for the first time in their private devotions; when they were wrapt up nearest to God, the Spirit took them, and made them to speak sometimes song, sometimes words, in a tongue; and by degrees, according as they sought more and more unto God, the gift became perfected, until they were moved to speak in tongues, even in the presence of others. In this stage I suffered them not to speak in the Church, according to the canon of the apostle; and even in private, in my own presence, I permitted it not; but I heard that it had been done. I would not have rebuked it; I would have sympathized tenderly with the person who was carried in the Spirit and lifted up; but in the Church I would not have permitted it. In the process of time, about fourteen days after, the gift perfected itself, so that they were made to speak in tongues, and prophesy the Word in English, for exhortation, edification, and comfort, which is the proper definition of prophecy, as testified by one of the witnesses."[1]

At first those who spoke with tongues did so pri-

[1] Mrs. Oliphant, *op. cit.*, p. 575.

vately, because restrained by Irving, but early in
November of the same year matters came to a crisis.
Notwithstanding his orders of prohibition of the use
of tongues in the public service, he was unexpectedly
interrupted during his sermon, and explanation had
to be made to the congregation. The matter was thus
taken out of Irving's hand by an occurrence which
was to him a visible sign of the will and pleasure of
God, to be restrained by him at his peril. As soon as
he was fully convinced that this was the work of the
Spirit, tongues and prophecy were to be heard at
every service.

It must be noticed that he made a distinction between the gift of tongues and that of prophecy. His
London address, referred to above, states this very
clearly. The speaking with tongues was usually short,
and was supposed to be a preliminary guarantee of
the authenticity of the prophecy which was to follow.
Irving says: "The apostle was here writing of speaking with tongues, in contradistinction to prophesying; that is to say, speaking nothing but the unknown tongue; for what should it profit unless there
be an interpreter? He is not speaking of what we
have; that which we have is one-fifth or one-tenth
in tongue, and the rest in prophesying. He is making
the distinction between speaking with tongues and
prophesying. No one in our Church could say the
person speaking is mad, because he doth not utter,

perhaps, more than two minutes or one minute in tongue, and then he begins to prophesy in English for the edification, exhortation, and comfort of all: the one is the sign of inspiration that it is the power of the Spirit; the other is the thing which the Spirit would give forth for the edification of the Church.

"Sometimes it comes forth without the sign, but generally it is otherwise; for I think I have observed in the Church, when many who are present disbelieve, or doubt, or mock, the sign is given in great power; but it is otherwise ordered in a company of persons believing the calling of the prophet, when the sign is not given but the word of prophecy comes out simply."[1]

In his dissertation on "The Interpretation of Tongues,"[2] he has the following in the same connection. "It [the interpretation of tongues] did not consist in their knowledge of the strange words, or the structure of the foreign languages. It was nothing akin to translation; the Spirit did not become a schoolmaster at all; but brought to the man's soul with the certainty of truth, that this which He was giving him to utter was the interpretation of the thing which the other had just spoken. This conviction might be brought to the spirit of the speaker himself, and then he was his own interpreter; but

[1] Mrs. Oliphant, *op. cit.*, p. 578.
[2] *Collected Writings of Edward Irving*, V, pp. 495 ff.

it was more frequent to bestow that gift upon another. This provision of an order who should interpret, as well as an order who should speak with tongues, shows that the gift of tongues had a higher origin than from the variety of languages amongst men. If it had been merely for preaching the truth to people of other languages, an order of interpreters would never have been required at all. If it had only been given for conveying the truth to foreign nations, then why have so many in each church, like the church of Corinth? . . . The unknown tongue, as it began its strange sounds, would be equal to a voice from the glory. 'Thus saith the Lord of hosts,' or 'This is my Son, hear ye him;' and every ear would say, 'Oh, that I knew the voice;' and when the man with the gift of interpretation gave it out in the vernacular tongue, we would be filled with an awe, that it was no other than God who had spoken it. . . . The strange tongue takes away all source of ambiguity, proving that the man himself hath nothing to do with it, and leaves the work and the authority of the work wholly in the hand of God. And therefore tongues are called a sign to the unbeliever."

Carlyle has expressed, in his letters, his opinion of the gift of tongues in no uncertain tones, especially as connected with Irving. Some extracts follow:

SPEAKING WITH TONGUES

(Letter to Mrs. Carlyle, August 15, 1831.)

"From all I can see, Irving seems to have taken his part: is forgotten by the intellectual classes, but still flourishes as a green bay-tree (or rather green cabbage-tree) among the fanatical classes, whose ornament and beacon he is. Strangely enough, it is all fashioned among these people; a certain everlasting truth, ever new truth, reveals itself in them, but with a body of mere froth and soap-suds and other like ephemeral impurities. Yet I love the man, and can trustfully take counsel of him. His wife I saw some nights ago—leaner, clearer-complexioned, I should say clearer-hearted, also, and clearer-headed; but alas! very straitlaced, and living in the suds element."[1]

(Letter to Mrs. Carlyle, August 22, 1831.)

"Friday I spent with Irving in the *animali parlanti* region of the supernatural. Understand, ladykin, that the 'gift of tongues' is here also (chiefly among the women), and a positive belief that God is still working miracles in the Church—by hysterics. Nay, guess my astonishment when I learned that poor Dow of Irongray is a wonder-worker and speaker with tongues, and had actually 'cast out a devil' (which, however, returned again in a week)

[1] J. A. Froude, *ibid.*, II, p. 174.

96

between you and Dumfries! I gave my wildest stare: but it is quite indubitable. His autograph letter was read to me, detailing all that the 'Laart' had done for him. . . . I was very wae for him, and not a little shocked. Irving hauled me off to Lincoln's Inn Fields to hear my double (Mr. Scott) where I sat directly behind a speakeress with tongues, who unhappily, however, did not perform till after I was gone. My double is more like 'Maitland,' the cotton-eared, I hope, than me; a thin, black-complexioned, vehement man, earnest, clear, and narrow as a tailor's listing. For a stricken hour did he sit expounding in the most superannuated dialect (of Chroist and so forth), yet with great heartiness the meaning of that one word Entsagen. The good Irving looked at me wistfully, for he knows I cannot take miracles in; yet he looks so piteously, as if he implored me to believe. Oh dear! oh dear! was the Devil ever busier than now, when the supernatural must either depart from the world, or reappear there like a chapter of Hamilton's *Diseases of Females?*"[1]

(Letter to Mrs. Carlyle, October 20, 1831.)

"I dare say you have not seen in the newspapers, but will soon see, something extraordinary about poor Edward Irving. His friends here are all much

---

[1] J. A. Froude, *ibid.*, II, p. 180.

grieved about him. For many months he had been puddling and muddling in the midst of certain insane jargonings of hysterical women and crack-brained enthusiasts, who start up from time to time in public companies, and utter confused stuff, mostly 'Ohs' and 'Ahs,' and absurd interjections about 'the body of Jesus'; they also pretend to 'work miracles,' and have raised more than one weak, bedrid woman, and cured people of 'nerves,' or, as they themselves say, 'cast devils out of them.' All of which poor Irving is pleased to consider as the 'work of the Spirit,' and to janner about at great length, as making his church the peculiarly blessed of Heaven, and equal to or greater than the primitive one at Corinth. This, greatly to my sorrow and that of many, has gone on privately a good while, with increasing vigor; but last Sabbath it burst out publicly in the open church; for one of the 'Prophetesses,' a woman on the verge of derangement, started up in the time of worship, and began to speak with tongues, and, as the thing was encouraged by Irving, there were some three or four fresh hands who started up in the evening sermon and began their ragings; whereupon the whole congregation got into foul uproar, some groaning, some laughing, some shrieking, not a few falling into swoons; more like a Bedlam than a Christian church. Happily, neither Jane nor I was there, though we had been the previous day. We had not even heard of it. When going next evening to call on Irving, we found the house all decked out for a 'meeting,' (that is, about this same 'speaking with tongues'), and as we talked a moment with Irving, who had come down to us, there rose a shriek in the upper story of the house, and presently he exclaimed, 'There is one prophesying; come up and hear her!' We hesitated to go, but he forced us up into a back room, and there we could hear the wretched creature raving like one possessed: hooing, and haing, and talking as sensibly as one would do with a pint of brandy in his stomach, till after some ten minutes she seemed to grow tired and become silent.

"Nothing so shocking and altogether unspeakably deplorable was it ever my lot to hear."[1]

(Letter to Mrs. Carlyle, November 10, 1831.)

"Irving comes but little in our way; and one does not like to go and seek him in his own house in a whole posse of enthusiasts, ranters, and silly women. He was here once, taking tea, since that work of the 'Tongues' began. I told him with great earnestness my deep-seated, unhesitating conviction that it was no special work of the Holy Spirit, or of any spirit, save of that black, frightful, unclean one that dwells in Bedlam."[2]

[1] J. A. Froude, *ibid.*, II, pp. 219 ff.
[2] J. A. Froude, *ibid.*, II, p. 224.

SPEAKING WITH TONGUES

(Letter to John Carlyle, November 13, 1831.)

"As to Irving, expect little tidings of him. I think I shall henceforth see little of him. His 'gift of tongues' goes on apace. Glen says there was one performing yesterday; but, on the whole, the Cockneys are too old for such lullabies—they simply think he is gone distracted, or means to 'do' them."[1]

We can well see that notwithstanding Carlyle's love and respect for Irving he had not the least sympathy with the movement which became identified with the great preacher's name. Criticism, however, was not confined to the private letters of Irving's friends. The *Times* gave vent to some strong language on the subject. Among other things it said: "Are we to listen to the screaming of hysterical women and the ravings of frantic men? Is bawling to be added to absurdity, and the disturber of a congregation to escape the police and tread-mill because the person who occupies the pulpit vouches for his inspiration?"

Irving himself never spoke with tongues and really had little to do with the development of the Catholic Apostolic Church. He seems rather in the light of one who had kindled a flame, which once kindled is beyond his power to extinguish or control. In this strange drama he appears more than a spec-

---

[1] J. A. Froude, *ibid.*, II, p. 227.

tator and less than an actor. He was there listening
with fervent faith, trying the spirits with anxious
scrutiny, his own lofty mind bringing to the test a
kind of reason and proof of those phenomena which
were entirely beyond either proof or reason, both to
the ecstatics who received them unhesitatingly and
to the skeptics who could not receive them at all.
Constant, steadfast, and without vacillation, he went
upon his heroic way. The plaudits formerly so freely
heaped upon him were refused, and no new honor
came to him; rather the contrary. Other voices of
higher authority than his echoed within the walls
once consecrated to his voice, while he, the foremost
to believe, bowed his head, thanked God, and bade
his people listen to the utterances from heaven. He
had prayed and God had answered; he had tried the
spirits, and with solemn acclamations they had stood
the test and owned the Lord; and now, regardless
of suffering, opposition, and agony, his faith never
failed him. He was expelled from the Presbyterian
church, and this new denomination was formed. He
preached at the opening of the new church, October
24, 1831, but was frequently interrupted by those
who claimed that the Spirit inspired them to speak
with tongues. A few of the utterances on that occasion have been recorded and saved, among which are
the following, in which the "Ahs" and "Ohs" of which
Carlyle spoke are quite apparent. This, it must be

remembered, is classed as prophecy rather than as speaking with tongues.

Irving mentioned the church as barren, upon which a voice interposed,

"Oh, but she shall be fruitful, oh! oh! oh! she shall replenish the earth! Oh! oh! she shall replenish the earth and subdue it—and subdue it!"

A little further on another voice broke in as follows,

"Oh! you do grieve the Spirit—you do grieve the Spirit! oh! the body of Jesus is to be sorrowful in spirit! You are to cry to your Father—to cry, to cry in the bitterness of your souls! Oh! it is a mourning, a mourning, a mourning before the Lord—a sighing and a crying unto the Lord because of the desolations of Zion—because of the desolations of Zion!"

At the close of the sermon he spoke to those who wished to be admitted to the meeting, when a voice broke forth:

"Ah! be ye warned! be ye warned! Ye have been warned. The Lord hath prepared for you a table, but it is a table in the presence of your enemies. Ah! look you well to it! The city shall be builded—ah! every jot, every piece of the edifice. Be faithful each under his load—each under his load; but see that ye build with one hand, and with a weapon in the other. Look to it—look to it. Ye have been warned. Ah! Sanballat, Sanballat, Sanballat; the Horonite, the

Moabite, the Ammonite! Ah! confederate, confederate, confederate with the Horonite! Ah, look ye to it, look ye to it!"[1]

Notwithstanding his mysticism and belief in the works of the Spirit, Irving was undoubtedly the sanest person in the congregation on that occasion. His stay in the church was brief and stormy; soon he retired to Wales, then to Scotland, where failing health brought him to an early death in 1834.

The new church went on. An extensive formulary, and a hierarchy, founded on the book of Revelations, all the members of which had seats curiously arranged on a large platform, were a part of their cult. This together with the supposed spiritual gifts attracted the curious, and for a few years the church continued to flourish.

We are only interested here in that part of its history which has to do with speaking with tongues. Those who have written on behalf of the church claim that in its doctrines it recognized a distinction between the gift of foreign tongues as recorded in the early chapters of Acts, and that of speaking with tongues as referred to by Paul in I Cor. 14. The former they think of as unique, the latter as a more common phenomenon: the first was due to the special circumstances and missionary requirements, the

---

[1] Mrs. Oliphant, *The Life of Edward Irving*, pp. 307-309.

second was valuable for individual worship. The church claimed only to have power similar to the Corinthian church and not like that of Pentecost.

This distinction was a development, for in the early days of Irvingism the gift was considered some spoken language. At the trial before the Presbytery of London, Mr. Taplin was asked why he concluded the languages, said to have been spoken, to be the gift of tongues. He answered, "Because I believe it is the Spirit that speaketh them; and do you think, sir, that the Spirit speaketh a gibberish?" Irving himself says: "Most frequently the silence is broken by utterance in a tongue, and this continues for a longer or a shorter period, sometimes occupying only a few words, as it were filling the first gust of sound; sometimes extending to five minutes, or even more, of earnest and deeply-felt discourse, with which the heart and soul of the speaker is manifestly much moved to tears, and sighs, and unutterable groanings, to joy, and mirth, and exultation, and even laughter of the heart. So far from being unmeaning gibberish, as the thoughtless and heedless sons of Belial have said, it is regularly-formed, well-proportioned, deeply-felt discourse, which evidently wanteth only the ear of him whose native tongue it is, to make it a very masterpiece of powerful speech." Mrs. Oliphant also says, "Mary Campbell herself expressed her conviction that the tongue given to her

was that of the Pelew Islands, which, indeed, was a
safe statement, and little likely to be authoritatively
disputed: while some other conjectures pointed to
the Turkish and Chinese languages as those thus miraculously bestowed. Since then opinion seems to
have changed, even among devout believers in these
wonderful phenomena; the hypothesis of actual languages conferred seems to have given way to that
of a supernatural sign and attestation of the intelligi-
ble prophecy, which, indeed, the Pentecostal experience apart, might very well be argued from St.
Paul's remarks upon this primitive gift."

"The character of the sound itself has perhaps received as many different descriptions as there are
persons who have heard it. To some, the ecstatic exclamations, with their rolling syllables and mighty
voice, were imposing and awful; to others it was
merely gibberish shouted from stentorian lungs; to
others an uneasy wonder, which it was a relief to
find passing into English, even though the height
and strain of sound were undiminished. One witness
speaks of it as 'bursting forth,' and that from the
lips of a woman, 'with an astonishing and terrible
crash'; another (Mr. Baxter), in his singular narrative, describes how, when 'the power' fell suddenly
upon himself, then all alone at his devotions, 'the utterance was so loud that I put my handkerchief to
my mouth to stop the sound, that I might not alarm

the house'; while Irving himself describes it with all his usual splendor of diction as follows:

" 'The whole utterance, from the beginning to the ending of it, is with a power, and strength, and fullness, and sometimes rapidity of voice altogether different from that of the person's ordinary utterance in any mood; and I would say, both in its form and in its effect upon a simple mind, quite supernatural. There is a power in the voice to thrill the heart and overawe the spirit after a manner which I have never felt. There is a march, and a majesty, and a sustained grandeur in the voice especially of those who prophesy, which I have never heard even a resemblance to, except now and then in the sublimest and most impassioned moods of Mrs. Siddons and Miss O'Neil. It is a mere abandonment of all truth to call it screaming or crying; it is the most majestic and divine utterance which I have ever heard, some parts of which I have never heard equalled, and no part of it surpassed, by the finest execution of genius and art exhibited at the oratorios in the concerts of ancient music. And when the speech utters itself in the way of a psalm or spiritual song, it is the likest to some of the most simple and ancient chants in the cathedral service, insomuch that I have often been led to think that those chants, of which some can be traced up as high as the days of Ambrose, are recollections and transmissions of the inspired utterances in the primitive Church."[1]

"The sound of the 'tongue' differed according to the character of the speaker, as they were stern, or gentle, or refined. Thus one ear-witness speaks of 'the beauty and regularity and majesty of some of the sounds.' Another speaks of a female 'who jabbered and gabbled at the height of her voice, in a tongue truly unknown, the vocables sounding, as if irreducible to grammatical construction, and mere contorted varieties of odd and fantastic syllables.' The first sound of another was generally a cry of great distress, loud, piercing, and a convulsive sob, and then a few words of Scripture said rapidly in a very powerful, strong voice, and often repeated over and over again; or words of reproach, entreaty, or command. There was something unnatural in the strength of voice for a woman. Mr. Taplin always, or almost always, began in a tongue which was a succession of sounds uttered in a most rapid manner. There was always something peculiarly unpleasant in his manner and excitement."

Mr. Pilkington, who was for some time a follower of Mr. Irving, set down various sounds which he declares he heard. Of one he says, that "it burst forth with an astonishing and terrible crash." He further

---

[1] Mrs. Oliphant, *op. cit.*, pp. 430 ff.

says, "that it gives some idea of the sound with which the tongue was delivered by him (Mr. Taplin), if cras-cran cra-crash were uttered with a sudden and rapid vociferation." The effect he describes to be such, that a lady, who herself was supposed to speak in the tongue, "although accustomed to it at a distance, involuntarily started three inches from her seat," when it was spoken alone to her.

Mr. Pilkington noted down other sounds which he heard, being the whole or part of what was supposed to be spoken in an unknown tongue. Such were "gthis dil emma sumo," "hozeghin alta stare," "holimoth holif aw thaw," "hezehamenanostra" three time repeated; "casa sera hastha caro, yeo cogo nomo." He explains some of these words as broken English, "holimoth holif aw thaw," being "Holy Most Holy Father"; (the last divided differently and pronounced broadly). The speaker did not deny that she had spoken in English, but whispered to her neighbor, "I didn't speak in English, did I?" Again, Mr. Taplin acknowledged Mr. Pilkington's translation of words which he himself had used, "contemn opposition," to have been correct. On his interpreting the words "gthis dil emma sumo" (preceded by some others, not imitable by orthography) "I will this dilemma assume," the speaker subsequently denied having uttered the word "dilemma." Now, had the words been (as was said) not understood by the speaker, she could not have remembered whether she had or had not uttered certain sounds. It would be most difficult for a person to remember a set of sounds, to which he had attached no meaning, and which had only once been uttered.

Mary Campbell not only spoke with tongues but wrote down what she intended for characters representing sounds. These fragments of writing were submitted to a number of persons, among whom were Dr. Lee, the Hebrew Professor at Cambridge, and Sir G. Staunton. Everyone knows the characters of many more languages than he is actually acquainted with, but these were not recognized. These characters were plainly not any known characters, but had most likeness to those which one sees on Chinese tea-chests, some memory of which was probably unconsciously retained by Mary Campbell when she made these marks.

A witness to the phenomena of the early days of the church gives the following description of them: " 'Before the outbreak of the discourse the person concerned appeared to be entirely sunk in reflection, his eyes closed and covered with the hand. Then suddenly, as if by an electric shock, he fell into a violent convulsion, which shook his whole frame. Upon this an impetuous gush of strange, energetic tones, which sounded to my ears most like those of the Hebrew language, poured from his quivering lips. This was

commonly repeated three times, and, as already remarked, with incredible vehemence and shrillness.
This first effusion of strange sounds, which were regarded chiefly as proof of the genuineness of the inspiration, was always followed, in the same vehement tone, by a longer or shorter address in English,
which was likewise repeated, some of it word by
word, and some sentence by sentence. It consisted
now of very pressing and earnest exhortations, now
of fearful warnings, containing, also, truly valuable
and moving words of consolation. The latter part
was usually taken to be an expository paraphrase of
the first, though it could not be decidedly explained
as such by the speaker. After this utterance, the inspired person remained a long time sunk in deep
silence, and only gradually recovered from the exhaustion of the effort.' The inward state of such persons was thus described to the narrator by a young
female: 'The Spirit fell upon her unawares and with
irresistible power. For the time she felt herself guided
and borne entirely by a higher power, without which
she would have been absolutely incapable of such
exertions. Of what she felt compelled to utter, she
had no clear consciousness; much less did she understand anything she spoke in a strange language,
entirely unknown to her; so that she could not afterwards tell definitely anything she had said. The utterance was invariably followed by great weariness

and exhaustion, from which she in a short time recovered.' "[1]

Mr. Baxter, one of Mr. Irving's principal followers and prophets who afterward recanted, tells us in his curious *Narrative of Facts*[2] his own experience concerning the gift. Among other things he says: "There was in me at the time of the utterance very great excitement, and yet I was distinctly conscious of a power acting upon me beyond the mere power of excitement. So distinct was this power from the excitement, that in all my trouble and doubt about it I never could attribute the whole to excitement. . . . The power fell upon me, and I was made to speak; and for two hours or upward the power continued upon me; and I gave forth what we all regarded as prophecies concerning the church and nation. . . . The power which then rested upon me was far more mighty than before, laying down my mind and body in perfect obedience, and carrying me on without confusion or excitement; excitement there might appear to a bystander, but to myself it was calmness and peace. Every former visitation of the power had been very brief; but now it continued, and seemed to rest upon me all the evening. The

[1] P. Schaff, *History of the Apostolic Church*, pp. 198 f.

[2] The full title is—*Narrative of Facts, characterizing the Supernatural Manifestations in Members of Mr. Irving's Congregation, and other Individuals in England and Scotland, and formerly in the Writer himself*, by Robert Baxter, 1833.

things I was made to utter flashed in upon my mind without forethought, without expectation, and without any plan or arrangement—all was the work of the moment, and I was as the passive instrument of the power which used me."

Schaff tells of his personal experience and that of a friend in the following words: "Several years ago I witnessed this phenomenon in an Irvingite congregation in New York; the words were broken, ejaculatory and unintelligible, but uttered in abnormal, startling, impressive sounds, in a state of apparent unconsciousness and rapture, and without any control over the tongue, which was seized as it were by a foreign power. A friend and colleague (Dr. Briggs), who witnessed it in 1879 in the principal Irvingite church at London, received the same impression."

CHAPTER VII

MODERN MANIFESTATIONS

MANY isolated examples of speaking with tongues might be given, extending down through the ages; but to show that it is still common, phenomena experienced in this century only will be discussed in this chapter. This will be in no wise an exhaustive list, but only a few incidents of many, simply as an indication of the present belief in this expression of spiritual power. Needless to say, the form reported by creditable witnesses is that of the Corinthian church rather than that of Pentecost.

In most cases the appearance of speaking with tongues has been connected with revival experiences or some other circumstances of a highly emotional character. At the beginning of this century there was a religious revival which nearly encircled the globe. It began in 1901 in Australia, was reported to England where similar experiences were sought, and in mission circles of India a determined effort was made to duplicate the Australian revival. In 1904 came the Welsh revival, in which the excess of emotion was discharged mostly by singing, but which had an important influence on the Welsh missions of India, and some impressive examples of speaking with tongues were reported from the last-named country.

The revival in Wales produced some examples of speaking with tongues. The following paragraph from the *Yorkshire Post* of December 27, 1904, is of interest in this connection: "Now comes the remarkable—in a sense the most remarkable—feature of the present revival. These young Welshmen and Welshwomen, who know little or no Welsh, and who certainly cannot carry on a sustained conversation in their parents' tongue, and who are supposed to have derived little or no benefit from the Welsh services, now, under the influence of the revival, voluntarily take part in public prayer,—but the language employed is almost invariably not the familiar English; but the unknown, or supposed to be unknown, Welsh Biblical phrases, and the peculiar idiomatic expression connected with a Welsh prayer which they never used before, and which they were supposed hitherto not to be able to understand, trip off their tongues with an ease and an aptness which might be supposed to indicate long and familiar usage. It is true these, as spoken, bear the unmistakable stamp of the English accent, but they also bear the equally unmistakable stamp of intelligent familiarity in their use.

"How is this to be accounted for? How can we explain the fact that a youth or maiden who cannot speak a dozen words in Welsh in ordinary conversation can nevertheless engage for five or ten minutes in public prayer in idiomatic Welsh? Do these young people really know Welsh without being conscious that they do know it? Have the religious services of the past after all appealed to an intelligence, the existence of which they themselves never suspected?

"There is thus opened up a very interesting study in psychology which, when explained, may help to explain also other features of the revival."

At Mukti, India, a high caste widow, named Pandita Ramabai, had an important educational and industrial work among women and girls. When she heard of the revival in other countries she organized prayer circles among the girls, so that in 1905 she had over five hundred girls so organized. These girls not only met in prayer circles, but some of them began to preach in the near-by villages. In 1907 speaking in tongues occurred and continued for some time. Mr. W. T. Ellis reports a scene witnessed by him at Mukti, where, at his own request, he was permitted to be present at a prayer meeting of one of the circles. About thirty girls were gathered together in a large bare room with a cement floor. All was confusion; the girls were praying aloud, some of them shouting at the top of their voices. Some of the girls were sitting on their feet with shoulders swaying and bodies jerking, while the faces of others betokened extreme agony. These young women were praying for and expecting a blessing in the form of Pentecostal gifts, and it is not surprising that speaking with tongues appeared.

Pandita Ramabai said to Mr. Ellis, "I've heard girls who don't understand English utter nice prayers in your language. I have heard others praying in Greek, Hebrew, and Sanskrit, and still others in languages which nobody among us understood. Some nights ago one of my girls prayed in this room and although she isn't advanced as far as the second grade, she prayed so clearly and nicely in English that the other teachers wondered who thus prayed. One girl is said in a trance state to have sung unknown songs in a low voice. . . . Other educated women and girls talked in English, and some used other languages which nobody among us in Kedgaon understood. That was no gabbling but very much like speaking in strange tongues, although I didn't understand it."[1]

In America, as well as in other countries, these phenomena occurred in their most extreme form. From the number of similar abnormal expressions which had already appeared in this country, especially from the time of the Kentucky revival down to the present century, it might have been prognosticated that this would be fertile soil. Numerous

[1] W. T. Ellis, "Have gift of tongues," *Chicago Daily News*, Jan. 14, 1908.

"Pentecostal Bands" and "Apostolic Gifts Societies" have appeared from time to time, in different parts of the country, and, after local notice and a momentary sensation, have disappeared. Influenced by this world-wide revival, the Apostolic Faith Movement began in 1910 and spread widely over the United States, being prominent in Los Angeles, California, where it is said by some that it began.[1] According to another account, Miss Ozman, a member of a Bible School in Topeka, Kansas, founded by an evangelist, Charles F. Parkham, received the gift of the Holy Spirit, and began to speak in tongues. A few days later several other students from the same school followed her example, and from here the above-named movement started.[2]

Both religious and secular newspapers and periodicals devoted considerable space to the manifestations of the members of this movement: it was real news, for it was extraordinary and seemed to be a special exhibition of divine power and a proof of divine favor. This advertising helped to spread the movement and to continue the manifestations. Those who believed in it claimed that speaking in tongues was the only evidence of the baptism of the Holy Spirit which the Bible gave. The glossolalics among

[1] D. A. Hayes, *The Gift of Tongues*, p. 85.
[2] A. E. Seddon, "Edward Irving and Unknown Tongues," *Homiletic Review*, 57, p. 108.

them said that the Holy Spirit took possession of their vocal organs and used them as he willed, while their minds were at rest. The last part of this statement will probably not be denied. While they knew their vocal organs were being used, they did not know what they were saying, and they were unable to stop speaking when the Spirit possessed them.

There seems to have been a very active branch of this movement in Chicago, and several writers have given us accounts of meetings which they attended there. While details differ in accounts of any two or more meetings, the general description is much the same. The meetings began with singing, praying, and testimonies, increasing gradually in loudness and excitement until motor automatisms appeared in the form of jerking of the body, high jumping, loud shouting, and then speaking with tongues. Accompanying these were sometimes sensory automatisms in the form of visions and hallucinations of hearing. The excitement was often at its height during prayer, and waves of ecstasy seemed to appear in the assembly. Not infrequently some member of the congregation fell to the floor unconscious, and if one form of physical manifestation appeared in a meeting or among the members of a congregation, it was spread through the well-known phenomenon of psychic contagion, so that it became common. All of these automatisms were considered to be special favors of God and proofs of the workings of the Spirit.

The visions which these people reported were naturally of various kinds. Sometimes they were of Jesus or of the apostles, or perhaps of flowers or birds—the dove as a symbol of the Spirit was not uncommon. Bright lights were also reported, which readily changed to tongues of fire, to accord with the experience at Pentecost. Sometimes the vision was symbolic, and was interpreted by someone else present, or by an explaining voice which was heard only by the one receiving the vision. Coupled with other experiences there were sometimes reported cases of healing, and the conditions were such that we might expect this, for the subjects were most favorably conditioned for the acceptance of suggestions of any kind, especially those of mental healing. These people were consistent in this much that they claimed all the power of the Spirit as recorded in the New Testament, and every form of manifestation of this power was prayed for, expected, and attempted.

In the meetings in which there was speaking with tongues among the people who claimed this and other Pentecostal gifts, the approach of the second coming of Jesus was usually a prominent tenet and subject for discourse. Sometimes the exact day was set for the advent, and at times people were encouraged to dispose of property and to make other preparations for the end of the world. Closely connected with this, and at times a part of this, was the prophecy of future events; and a supernormal knowledge of events which were happening at a distance was claimed.

One could hardly ask for a more favorable environment for the appearance of speaking with tongues. The expectation, the suggestion, the high pitch of emotion, the encouragement to testify,—all the conditions favored an inhibition of rational expression and an automatic movement of the organs of speech. Those who attended the meetings for purposes of investigation testified to the almost irresistible character of the contagion and the ease with which this gift appeared and continued. In truth, it seemed to be one of the freest outlets for the high head of emotion. The fact that it was accepted at its face value, and received as a special mark of favor, increased the frequency of this form of manifestation.

Not only did persons speak in tongues, but reports from China, India, and America contain accounts of persons normally unable to sing, who, when in a state of ecstasy, sang harmoniously in tongues. This ability was portrayed in "Trilby." As a further example, Pastor Paul sang familiar hymns in tongues. The glossolalic version of the hymn, "Let me go," was as follows:

"schua ea, schua ea,
O tschi biro ti ra pea
akki lungo tari fungo
u li bara ra tungo
latschi bungo ti tu ta."

"Anyone can see," said Paul, "how remarkably these words rhyme. And what is more remarkable, there is more rhyme in this song in tongues than in the German words. When I made this discovery, I could not but praise God." Some songs given to him in tongues he was unable to understand. Edward Irving testified that the singing in the Spirit, which was a part of the experience in his church, seemed to him to embody more than earthly music and to be the primary type of religious music, of which all chants and hymns were but faint and poor echoes. What is called by some "writing in tongues" was simply the familiar phenomenon of automatic writing, but with the use of unfamiliar characters. A very good example of this will be seen in the next chapter when we examine the writing of Mlle. Smith in Martian characters. Usually the characters were made as bizzare as possible to prove their difference from the characters commonly used by the writer.

The people who have been the most successful in speaking with tongues have usually been those who were earnest and devout, but uneducated and not very intelligent. This is not always the case, however. Consider, for instance, this testimony from Pastor Barratt of Norway, quoted by Professor Henke. "I am a minister of twenty years' standing in the Methodist Episcopal Church and would sooner die than give way to humbug. I know that what the Pentecost God gave me is the same kind of blessing as that received by the disciples at Pentecost in Jerusalem, and that the gift of tongues to me is as pure as the gift spoken by Paul to the Corinthians. And I know that numbers are now rejoicing in this blessing all over Scandinavia. The tongues of fire have been seen over our heads by Christians and worldly people alike, the sound of a rushing mighty wind (no delusion) has been heard by numbers, visions and trances have also been enjoyed by many, but best of all is that the love of God burns like a holy flame in the hearts of thousands who are willing to go to the stake for Christ."[1]

Some people, like Irving, have sought the gift but failed to receive it. A certain type of temperament is also necessary for success, as well as a large amount of credulity. Usually, too, the scriptural basis of the religious life of these people is confined to a few passages often repeated, and favorable to some extraordinary manifestation.

[1] F. G. Henke, "The Gift of Tongues," etc., *American Journal of Theology*, 13, p. 196.

Regarding the glossolalics in Chicago one observer said: "The most of the people affected were foreigners, and, if I could judge correctly from their appearance and accent, they were Norwegians and Swedes. The most of them were quite intelligent and respectable in outward seeming, and would have sat in any ordinary religious congregation without attracting attention by any peculiarity of feature or dress. There were some, however, who seemed fit candidates for an insane asylum, evidently with small mentality and on the edge of nervous wreck. All seemed to belong to the working class, and there was an unusual proportion of middle-aged and elderly, fleshy women who appeared to be matrons and housekeepers from humble homes, and who probably found the only excitement in their humdrum existence in these services."[1]

Another observer said: "The origin of these meetings was among people such as were generally found in the mission houses of Chicago: people of the lower classes, especially foreigners. In one place there were Italians, in another one Swedes and Germans. The whole meeting was very exciting, and it need hardly be mentioned that there was little spiritual food for an advanced Christian."

Not infrequently some of those who speak in tongues are not only positive that they are speaking

[1] D. A. Hayes, *The Gift of Tongues*, p. 87.

a real language but are so sure that they designate the language used. Some, who think that the gift of tongues at Pentecost was given to the apostles to be used for the ready spread of the gospel, consider the gift to themselves for the analogous use in missionary service. So far as careful investigation has been able to determine, no cases have been known where the gift was ever used for this purpose by missionaries, and certainly the apostles did not use it in this way. The *Baptist Argus,* of Louisville, Kentucky, January 23, 1908, published the results of an investigation of a number of cases in which definite claims were made; some of these I quote:

"I have been asked about a certain Mr. McIntosh. Notwithstanding that he expected to preach at once to the people, he has been wholly unable to do so. He must not only have an interpreter in preaching but also in the simplest affairs of everyday life. From the day of his arrival in China until now neither he nor his wife has been able to speak; I speak not from rumor but from personal knowledge, and the personal admission of failure by Mr. McIntosh himself.

"As to Japan, while there I met a party of about a dozen missionaries who had come out from the state of Washington on the Pacific Coast. I visited them in their homes and attended one of their services. They too expected to speak at once to the people, but on reaching Japan they were powerless to do so. They admitted to me their inability, and I saw it with my own eyes.

"As to India, you remember that Rev. A. G. Garr and wife went there also expecting to preach to the people in this supernatural way. But did they? They have now left India and are in Hongkong. I have attended two of their services. Mr. Garr in reply to a personal question of mine as to whether either he or his wife had been able to talk in the native language of India, said that they have been unable to do so.

"Again, two ladies came on from the Japan party to Hongkong because they felt they had the gift of the 'Hongkong dialect.' I have seen them, inquired of their power to talk in Chinese and they too were unable to speak."

Reverend Mr. Seddon said: "I have never yet heard any other than the English language. Some groaned and shouted incoherencies I have heard, but to my ears these bear no resemblance to language as spoken between men in the common affairs of life. I claim some qualifications to judge in this matter, having knowledge of eight languages, some of which have been learned during residence in the countries where they are spoken. If any of these had been used, I could have instantly detected it."[1]

[1] A. E. Seddon, "Edward Irving and Unknown Tongues," *Homiletic Review,* 57, p. 108.

The experience of some glossolalics may be enlightening. After reading of the gift of tongues in Norway and in America, and seeing the statement that no one could be sure he was baptized with the Spirit unless he spoke with tongues, Pastor Paul "strove with his whole heart" for the gift, spending whole nights in prayer. Finally, "on the 15th of September, in the forenoon meeting the power of the Lord came upon me and continued its work on my body throughout the whole day, as often as I was in the meeting. . . . In the evening we (seven brethren together) had another prayer meeting. Between 10 and 11 o'clock the effect on my mouth was so strong that my lower jaw, tongue and lips moved as if to speak, without any effort on my part. I was fully conscious at the time, entirely at rest in the Lord, deeply happy, and I let all this happen without being able to speak. Even if I attempted to pray aloud I could not, for none of my German words fitted into the position of my mouth. Likewise no words of any other language I knew fitted the positions which my mouth now assumed. I thus saw that my mouth was speaking silently in a strange tongue; and I perceived that it would yet be given to me to utter words correspondingly. About 11 o'clock most of the gathering returned to their homes, especially such as had to go to work early in the morning; and thus there only remained with me two brethren, of whom one was Rev. H. When we prayed my mouth again began to move, and I noticed that all I lacked was the ability to give sounds to the movements of my lips. I looked up to the Lord that he might vouchsafe it and soon I was moved to speak. But now something wonderful happened. It seemed as if a new organ was forming in my lungs which brought about sounds that would fit into the position of my mouth. Since the movements of the mouth were very rapid, this had to happen very quickly. In this way a wonderful language arose in sounds that I had never spoken before. I had the impression according to the tones, that it might be Chinese. Then came an entirely different language with an entirely different position of the mouth and wonderful sounds. Because we had just had missionary meetings that day on behalf of China and the South-Sea Islands I naturally thought it might be a South-Sea language. I do not know how long I spoke thus—surely some minutes. Then I had to break out in German in praise and worship of my God. I was sitting during all this, nevertheless my body was shaken by a great power, though in nowise unpleasant or painful."

Barratt, one of the principal representatives of the Pentecostal movement in Germany, thus reports his experience: "I got up from my lying position continually speaking in new language. I spoke at least eight different languages that night. How could I know that they were different languages? I felt that the position of the mouth was different. The power took my lower jaw and my tongue and forced the languages out clear and distinct while nothing kept the power back in me. Once my wind pipe hurt me. I think at that time it was Gaelic. I know that language. Another time there were nasal sounds, probably French. I am sure that I spoke Italian."

The description of the case of Rev. E. A. Street may be briefly summarized. This minister prayed for twelve years for a Pentecostal experience, reaching as a climax a condition in which he frequently spent until five o'clock in the morning in prayer. Though he reached, as he believed, the valley of humiliation and became empty of thought, he did not receive the gift, but encouraged by those of the Apostolic Mission (Chicago) continued to wait and pray, and the answer finally came in the form of uncontrollable laughter—drunken with the "new wine." After varying experiences of laughter, groanings and unconsciousness, he began to speak "baby gibberish," words of Chinese and various things in strange tongues. A day or two later he was awakened from sleep and sang "heavenly music" at the top of his voice. After prayer for the power of interpretation, he was answered and became able to interpret his own, or others' "tongues," simply by requesting the power to do so! It should be mentioned that in addition to his own intense longings and incessant praying, the advice and the laying on of the hands of the mission leader, Elder Sinclair, preceded these experiences.[1]

Some more recent experiences may be quoted. "Well, thank God, that night I did lose my own mind, and the mind of the Lord came in. Oh glory! I tarried until, and with me it was 2:15 in the morning of September 6, 1921, when it seemed to me as though an awful electric storm had broken loose and I was hit by all God's lightning, for when the fire fell I saw it, and it hit me and knocked me over on my back and I burst out speaking in tongues, praise the Lord, as He gave utterance. For two hours I was under the power, praising the Lord in a new tongue."[2]

"Elder Schwab of Wesley Temple, Winnipeg, Manitoba, sends in this news in a recent letter: 'You remember little Dolly, whom you said was such an inspiration to you at the children's meetings on Saturday afternoon. She was in the prayer room very earnestly praying. She apparently has never been very satisfied in regard to the Baptism with the Holy Spirit, and whilst she was engaged in prayer, all of a sudden she started to pray in another language.

[1] "Pentecostal Experience of Rev. E. A. Street," *Intercessory Missionary*, June 1907.
[2] *The Pentecostal Evangel*, Aug. 11, 1923.

Harry Mah, one of our Chinese Crusader boys, was right close by her, when all of a sudden we noticed him staring at her with his eyes and mouth wide open, and in a few moments he turned round and said to me, "She is speaking in Chinese." I said, "What is she saying?" He said, "She says that Jesus is coming again; get ready." He said she continued to speak in Chinese for a considerable time, when all of a sudden she started singing. Harry says, "Listen! She is singing a Chinese song, one that I have learned in the Chinese Y. M. C. A." He was full of excitement, and said, "I have never heard a foreigner speak such good Chinese."

" 'After the after-meeting was over, he questioned her, and wanted to know if she had ever heard anyone sing that Chinese hymn, but the girl did not know a word of Chinese. Then Harry started to sing the same hymn himself, which he had learned at the Y. M. C. A. You can rest assured that this proved a great blessing to everyone present, to see God confirming His Word in such a way.' "[1]

In an account of his being captured by bandits in China on January 15, 1926, Thomas Hindle said: "While seated on the kang, I prayed aloud in Chinese and the power of God's Holy Spirit came over me. I shook under the power and prayed in

[1] *The Pentecostal Evangel*, Dec. 5, 1925, quoting *Revival Broadcast*.

tongues. My captors were visibly affected. Ye who have no use for 'manifestations' consider this case. The chief . . . ordered me to stop, but though willing to do so I could not wholly obey. Presently one of them said to me, 'You can go now.' I thanked him and went to the door."[1]

Almost invariably, as we might naturally suppose, speaking with tongues is considered the work of the Holy Spirit. The following recent incident is an exception. "I attended the 'Tongues' meeting at H——. Here I found men and women lying on the floor in all shapes, and the workers would put big blankets over them. These people on the floor would be jabbering all at once in what they called unknown tongues. While I was praying one of the workers got hold of me and said: 'Holy Ghost, we command thee to go into this soul.' The workers were jabbering and shaking their hands over me, and a hypnotic power (as I know now) took possession of me, and I fell among the people on the floor and knew nothing for ten hours. When I came to my senses I was weak and my jaws were so tired they ached. I believed that this power was of God. They said I was wonderfully blest, and Rev. W—— sent me from one place to another so that I could jabber in tongues. I was told that while I was speaking in tongues the people would fall on their faces and say 'Yes, Lord,'

[1] *The Pentecostal Evangel,* March 20, 1926.

'We will, Lord,' thinking it was God who was speaking through me."[1] The writer subsequently considered speaking in tongues the work of demons.

As this book is going through the press, there appears on the front page of a New York daily paper an account of speaking with tongues in a prominent New York City church. The pastor of this church, in an interview printed in this paper, explained that, in a prayer meeting held in his church, his son was overcome by a power which he believed to be the baptism of the Holy Spirit. Quoting the pastor, this paper continues: "He was kneeling at the time this experience came to him, and others were kneeling. He was kneeling by a chair, and in prayer. He was overcome, and he fell to the floor. And his mother and I heard him singing in a most beautiful way while this power was upon him. There was a rhythm to his singing, and it was very beautiful, although he was singing in an unknown language. His face was illumined with joy." Three days before this account appeared, the same paper contained an editorial on a Kentucky sect designated, "The Unknown Tongue."[2] Items of this kind appearing somewhat frequently show that speaking with tongues continues to be a modern religious manifestation.

In all these cases there is no reason to think that

[1] A. White, *Demons and Tongues*, p. 60.
[2] *The New York Times*, June 21, 24, and 25, 1927.

either the glossolalics themselves or the witnesses were dishonest in asserting that words of foreign languages were repeated. It is difficult to give utterance to a number of nonsense syllables without some one syllable or more bearing some resemblance to syllables of some foreign language, and the stress of the excitement adds to the suggestion of still other likenesses. The practical test of speaking with persons familiar with a language of which knowledge is claimed has, in the past, usually resulted disastrously.

There seems to be a great difference in individuals concerning the time necessary for incubation. For example, a speaker in tongues told a girl of fifteen she would receive the gift of tongues. In the next meeting she spoke freely and not only there but in her home she could not restrain the glossolalic expression. In contrast with this, Barratt had to wait thirty-nine days, praying and wrestling, before he received it. During this time he experienced convulsive movements of the throat and jaws at intervals until he was successful. In addition to other means for bringing about the result, he tried laying on of hands and copied other apostolic methods.

Among the spiritual gifts in the Chicago meetings, that of interpretation of tongues was not lacking. In some cases the leader of the meeting—one who was acting as pastor in charge of the mission—did most of it. After the glossolalic had finished his speaking, the leader sometimes came forward and repeated a passage of scripture, which he said was the interpretation of the unintelligible utterance to which the audience had just listened. Or instead of the scripture passage, it might be a denunciation of the scornful and unbelieving, or words of encouragement to the hesitating, or some other statement which he claimed was the message which had been given in unknown tongues. Sometimes the interpretation seemed more plausible than at others, for if the glossolalic, as it occasionally happened, simply repeated the same syllable over and over again, interpretation was a difficult task.

The practical importance of the Pentecostal gifts has been found quite negligible. The spiritual and physical benefits vary in amount and permanence with the individual. Beyond a doubt such extreme indulgences have unsettled many, and predisposed them to weakness and sin rather than to strength and godliness.

Another most unfortunate result is the division caused by the censoriousness with which those participating in the new faith regard other Christians, and by the suspicion and dislike with which they are themselves in turn regarded. Those who have claimed special spiritual gifts have also claimed exclusive possession of the truth, and they have exhibited a tendency to scold and denounce the absent church members and ministers as being destitute of the grace presumed to be possessed and exhibited by the members of this cult. Whatever else may be predicted concerning this gift, it seems certain that it is not decreed that the Christian faith shall be propagated in this way—or, indeed, that it ever has been.

CHAPTER VIII

NON-RELIGIOUS SPEAKING WITH TONGUES

WHILE speaking with tongues has been primarily a religious phenomenon, and, on account of the example and influence of Pentecost, principally associated with the Christian religion, it is by no means connected exclusively with Christianity or with other forms of religion. To show the more general character of the so-called marvel, two cases of a non-religious type, which have been thoroughly investigated, will be presented.

The first case will be that now somewhat celebrated one of Mlle. Hélène Smith (a pseudonym). Prof. Th. Flournoy, professor of psychology at the University of Geneva, observed and studied this case very thoroughly, and reported it in a volume entitled, *Des Indes à la Planète Mars*. This was subsequently translated into English, and published under the title, *From India to the Planet Mars*. It is from the English edition which I shall quote.

Hélène Smith was born in Geneva in 1864. Her father was a Hungarian and her mother a Swiss. Though a merchant, her father was a linguist of ability; he spoke Hungarian, German, French, Italian, Spanish, and English, and he knew Latin and

Greek. Her mother was somewhat mediumistic and had visions. The hereditary qualities from both sides of her family combined to produce the characteristics which Mlle. Smith exhibited. She was educated in the common schools, and between her ninth and twentieth years showed various automatisms. After leaving school she entered a business house where she was promoted to a responsible and important position. She was a beautiful woman, in splendid health, of irreproachable character, and carried her responsibilities in a most capable manner. She was perfectly normal in her ordinary state except for occasional visions of short duration.

In 1892 she became acquainted with spiritualists, developed mediumistic ability, and before long was the principal medium of the group, but always served without any remuneration. Her mediumship was visual, auditive, and by table tapping, and she was under the guidance of a spirit who called himself Leopold, but who was really Joseph Balsamo—the notorious Count Cagliostro. Up to the age of thirty her automatisms were conscious, but subsequently and more frequently she lost consciousness and failed to have recollections of what had transpired when she awoke. In other words, she experienced total somnambulism. Her trance states, which took place under the usual spiritualistic conditions, were rich in experiences, the reality of which was accepted by

Mlle. Smith as well as by others present, but which were explained according to current psychological theory by Professor Flournoy.

The organization of the trance states was very thorough. Their story may be epitomized as follows: Five hundred years before, she was the daughter of an Arab sheik, and became, under the name of Simandini, the favorite wife of a Hindoo prince. Being reincarnated, she reappeared in the person of the illustrious and unfortunate Marie Antoinette; again she reappeared as Hélène Smith. As a medium, she entered into relations with the people and affairs of Mars, as a reward and consolation for this life. In trance, she lived three distinct lives, the Hindoo, the Royal, and the Martian. It was in the last that fully developed speaking with tongues appeared, although there were some experiences of this character in the Hindoo, and some changes of spelling in her writing to conform to the purported time of the royal existence.

In 1895, a young man, seventeen years of age, named Alexis Mirbel, died. His mother attended a spiritualistic séance, at which Mlle. Smith was the principal medium, to endeavor to establish communication with him. In a trance, Mlle. Smith went to Mars and saw him there. Fifteen months later he again appeared speaking Martian, but did not understand French. However, he left Mars and upon entering inter-planetary space again used French. In February 1896, while in a trance state, a woman appeared to Mlle. Smith and wanted her to enter a curious little car without wheels or horses. The woman spoke a strange language, and Mlle. Smith, purporting to repeat it, recited an incomprehensible jargon. The trance then became complete; she took a journey to Mars and performed a complicated pantomime expressing the manners of Martian politeness. After awaking, the company spoke French to her, but she answered in a strange language, four words of which were then identified and translated. Judged by these four words, said Professor Flournoy, "the Martian language is only a puerile counterfeit of French, of which she preserves in each word a number of syllables and certain conspicuous letters."

The first recitation of words, referred to as an incomprehensible jargon, was never translated or identified, and seems to have been "a continuation of sounds uttered at random and without any real meaning," similar to the speaking with tongues at Corinth. The fact that she claimed to understand it was not unlike the ecstatic interpretation of tongues not uncommon at Corinth. It was not until seven months later that Martian was spoken and translated by her, the intervening time being employed in the subconscious fabrication of a language. One and one-half years after the first appearance, the Martian written characters were presented.

Sometimes Martian phrases were given to her of which she did not know the meaning, and later at another séance they would be translated. She did not know Martian in her normal state, but occasionally unconsciously wrote French words in Martian characters or while talking used Martian words. Martian characters were also interspersed in her normal French writing.

In her subconscious presentation of Mars and Martian objects and expressions, the endeavor seemed to have been to make everything different from corresponding mundane objects and experiences. This endeavor, however, was not successful; for the creative imagination is limited in its details to former experiences of the person imagining, and usually differs only in the way in which these details are composed. For example, in imagining a dragon, the head, body, and tail are well known, the imagination simply bringing them together in an unusual manner. This was clearly the case in the descriptions which Mlle. Smith gave of her visual and auditory experiences on Mars. Any modifications of earthly things were childish and concerned with minute details.

The language is, of course, the most interesting to us of all the trance products, and was, in fact, the

most wonderful of all the purported revelations.
These revelations were made in four different ways:
namely, *first,* verbo-auditive automatisms. These
were hallucinations of hearing, accompanying vision
in her waking state. At such times she wrote down,
either during the vision or immediately afterward,
the unintelligible sounds which she heard. During
the visions which she had at séances, she slowly repeated the words she heard without understanding
them, and the sitters made the best possible notes of
them. *Second,* vocal automatisms. The sitters gathered as much as possible of the strange words pronounced rapidly in her trance. A distinction must be
made between the relatively clear and brief phrases
which were later translated by Esenale (Alexis Mirbel), and the rapid and confused gibberish which
was never translated and probably had no meaning,
as it was only a pseudo-language. *Third,* verbo-visual
automatisms. These had to do with the written language and consisted of apparitions of strange and
unknown characters before her eyes when awake,
which she copied faithfully. *Fourth,* graphic automatisms. These consisted of writing, traced by the hand
of Mlle. Smith while completely entranced and incarnating a Martian personage.

The process of the fabrication of the Martian
language, performed unconsciously by Mlle. Smith,
seems to have consisted in taking certain French sen-

tences or phrases and replacing each word in them with some other word chosen at random. It is simply French with the sounds changed. The personal pronouns, articles, and possessive adjectives are analogous to French, and there are many other analogies. "The simple vowels of the Martian alphabet correspond exactly with the five French vowels, *a, e, i, o, u,* and have the same shades of pronunciation. The Martian *c* plays the triple part which it fulfils in French. The *s* has the same capricious character. . . . It is generally hard, but between two vowels it becomes soft like *z.*" Perhaps the most tell-tale likeness is the introduction of a useless letter in Martian to correspond to the French euphonic *t.*

> Martian—Kévi bérimir m hed
> French—Quand reviendra-t-il?
> English—When will he return?

The letter *m* has no reason for existence except as a slavish copy of the French letter *t.* Professor Flournoy seems to have proved conclusively the French origin of Martian.

He is, however, sufficiently just to point out the value and excellencies of Martian. It is undoubtedly a language, manufactured by an individual, and not simply a gibberish or jargon as in cases of religious speaking with tongues. Further, "First: It is a harmony of clearly articulated sounds, grouped so as to form words. Secondly: These words when pronounced express definite ideas. Thirdly: . . . Connection of the words with the ideas is continuous; . . . the significance of the Martian terms is permanent and is maintained . . . from one end to the other of the texts. . . . It has an acoustic quality altogether its own, due to the prominence of certain sounds, and has a peculiar intonation difficult to describe."

The ingenuity displayed by the Martian language consists of three peculiarities: namely, "1. In default of capitals, the initials of proper names are often distinguished by a point placed above the ordinary character.

"2. In the case of double letters the second is replaced by a point situated at the right of the first.

"3. Finally, there exists, in order to designate the plural of substantives and of some adjectives, a special graphic sign, answering to nothing in the pronunciation and having the form of a small vertical undulation."

I have already quoted Professor Flournoy's opinion of the Martian based on the first four words, and indicated it in other ways. Perhaps I should quote more definitely his mature opinion after a more complete analysis and investigation. "Martian is, in my opinion, only an infantile travesty of French."[1]

[1] Th. Flournoy, *From India to the Planet Mars*, p. 241.

"Martian is only disguised French."[1] "The Martian cycle, with its unknown language, evidently betrays an eminently puerile origin and the display of an hereditary linguistic aptitude, buried under Hélène's ordinary self."[2]

While the Martian is by far the most extensive and most important of Mlle. Smith's speaking with tongues, it does not comprehend all of it. After Professor Flournoy had criticized the Martian as being simply a counterfeited French, there was a subconscious attempt to fabricate another language, which was translated into Martian and from Martian into French, but it was altogether insignificant as compared with the Martian. During the Marie Antoinette trance experience there were simple changes in the spelling of French, the earlier *ois* being substituted for the later *ais;* this was of little importance. Perhaps more important, if much less extensive, was the Hindoo language, for this could be examined and compared to actual, spoken language.

Mlle. Smith seems to have possessed some subconscious knowledge of the customs and language of Eastern people, but, notwithstanding the most careful examination and investigations, Professor Flournoy was unable to trace the source of this knowledge. Her father at one time lived in Algeria,

---

[1] Th. Flournoy, *op. cit.,* p. 249.
[2] Th. Flournoy, *op. cit.,* p. 444.

but so far as could be ascertained had never communicated any of the language or customs of this country to his daughter. The most important production of her trance state was the writing of four words of Arabian text. She also seems to have used Sanscrit words a number of times. Her Hindoo seems to have been a mixture of improvised articulations and of veritable Sanscrit words adapted to the situation. Isolated Hindoo words were not uncommonly produced in auditive hallucinations, in automatic writing, and in words uttered in semi-somnambulism. On one occasion some were inserted in a Martian text.

M. de Glardon, to whom the supposed Hindoo was submitted for examination and opinion, declared that it was neither ancient nor modern Hindustani, but probably Sanscrit and invented words. M. Michel was of the opinion that it contained four fragments of Sanscrit well adapted to the situation. M. de Saussure said that it did not represent Sanscrit, but it was a medley of syllables, in the midst of which there were incontestably some series of eight or ten syllables, constituting a fragment of a sentence which had a meaning. The other syllables never had an anti-Sanscrit character. The value of the last statement, however, is considerably diminished by the fact that she seldom launched out with complicated forms of syllables and most commonly used the vowel *a* which in Sanscrit is employed four times to once of the other vowels. It is evident, also, that subconsciously she possessed a part, at least, of the Devanagari alphabet, but did not know the concrete use of it. Different from the Martian, there was never a word for word translation of the Hindoo, but there were only pantomimic or general and free translations, which lead one to think that her knowledge was not sufficient for a literal translation.

There were certain phenomena which Professor Flournoy noted, incident to her speaking in an unknown tongue, which link this experience with that of others. At one time Mlle. Smith spoke in verse, and said of it subsequently, "I do not know why I spoke those words; . . . I was obliged to speak them, I assure you, in spite of myself." The possession of the personality by some spiritual power, which New Testament and other religious glossolalics affirm, was paralleled in Mlle. Smith by the possession by her control—the spirit of Cagliostro or others. "After a series of hiccoughs, sighs, and various noises indicate the difficulty Leopold is experiencing in taking hold of the vocal apparatus, the words come forth slowly but strong." These same preliminary noises are not uncommon with other glossolalics, as we have seen in the former accounts. The voluble Martian utterances with which Mlle. Smith began her Martian speech were of the same character as the speaking with tongues most com-

146

monly used. They were simply a mass of meaningless syllables gushing forth under the control of the
excited lower centers. Of these, Professor Flournoy
says, "Simple, incoherent utterances, in a state of
ecstasy, interspersed with emotional exclamations,
. . . are met with in the dream, in somnambulism,
mental alienation, or in children."

The following reproductions may be of interest.

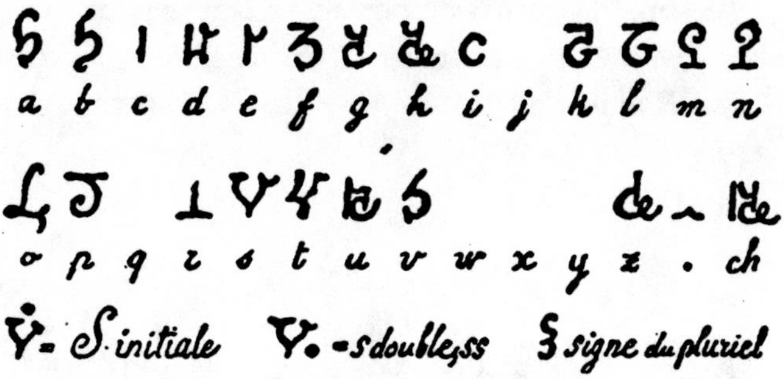

Fig. 24. Martian alphabet, summary of the signs
obtained. (Never has been given as such by Mlle.
Smith.) (P. 208.)

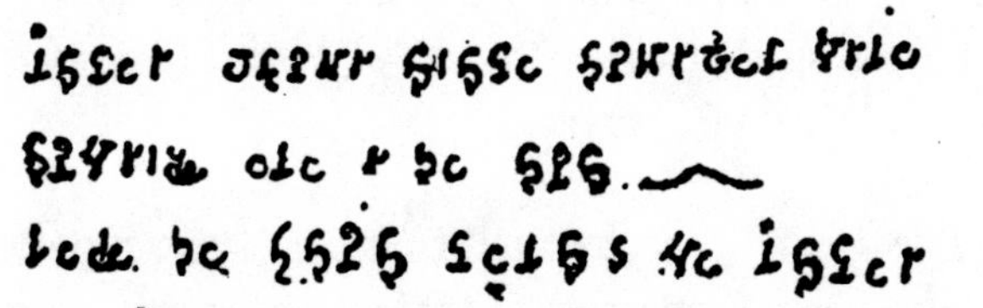

Fig. 32. Text No. 39 (April 1, 1899), written by
Mlle. Smith, incarnating Ramié.

147

39 Ramié   pondé   acâmi   andélir   téri
   Ramié, savant astronome, apparaîtra comme

antéch iri é vi   anâ.   riz vi banâ mirâ𝛏
hier souvent à toi maintenant. Sur toi trois adieux

ti Ramié ni Astané. évaï   divinée
de Ramié et Astané. Sois heureuse!

"Ramié, learned astronomer, will appear as yesterday often to thee now. Upon thee three adieux
from Ramié and Astané. Be happy!" (Pp. 239,
240.)

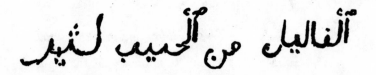

Fig. 35. Arabian text drawn from left to right by
Mlle. Smith in hemisomnambulism: elqalil men el-
habib ktsir, *the little from the friend (is) much.*
Natural size. (P. 312.)

The second case we shall consider is one reported
by the person who experienced it, an educated man
capable of examining critically and reporting dis-
criminatingly. The case, with an introduction by

148

Prof. William James and remarks by Mr. F. W. H. Myers, is to be found in the *Proceedings of the Society for Psychical Research*, Vol. XII, pp. 277 ff.

Mr. Albert LeBaron (a pseudonym), a literary man, aged thirty-nine, came to Professor James with an account of his experience. In connection with his literary work he had visited a shore resort where several mystics were spending the summer. These people were believers in and active participants in spiritualism. On a second visit he had experienced a vision and, following this, automatic movements and speech. Later there was speech in a strange voice and tone, but in the English language. According to the account of this experience, the voice was so like that of Miss J.'s deceased mother, who was supposed to have inspired the message, that the St. Bernard dog, which had been a special pet of the mother's, got up, went to him, and began to lap his hands as in recognition. Mr. LeBaron was so affected by the experience that he received it at its face value, accepting the prophetic words concerning his leadership which were automatically spoken. He was said to be the reincarnation of the Pharaoh of the Exodus whom Miss J.'s mother loved in a previous incarnation. One night he slept in the bed formerly occupied by the deceased father of the home. The next morning he awoke lame and limped for hours. He then discovered for the first time that the father had been lame. He had both visual and auditive hallucinations, seeing globules of light moving about the room and hearing raps on the headboard of his bed. A finger ring, supposed to possess occult powers, was loaned to him, and automatic writing was attempted. At first the movements were uncontrolled, but later he was successful.

He then became a devotee to spiritualism, and tried on every occasion to communicate with spirits, avoiding the living in order that he might have intercourse with the dead. He became ascetic, morbid on some subjects, and a believer in mystical religion of a spiritualistic type. Shortly after leaving the mystical group he received the following message, spoken automatically: "I am going to guide you into the way of truth. . . . You must be at the door of the church near the old home in the town of Stowe, which is in the state of Vermont, by the time the sun rises on next Tuesday. You will then see the reason why I told you to go." He did not know there was such a town as Stowe, but went according to directions and received a message of general import, indicating that he should be blessed. He received other messages of a general but inspiring nature and one telling him definitely of his incarnation.

On one morning came a message directing him to go to St. Louis to a certain street address. He went but found there a business address. Later, however, he went to a spiritualist in that city and received a message in a strange tongue, which was subsequently translated and proved to be a statement regarding incarnation and a message of inspiration. That night he received another inspiring message by automatic writing and also one spoken. On his return trip from St. Louis he had his first hallucination of hearing definite words spoken. He had many other directions to make long trips which he did not obey.

Shortly after his return from St. Louis he had his first experience in speaking in an unknown tongue, at his residence in a New York suburb. Of this he says: "Suddenly, whilst conversing with it [the psycho-automatism] in my bedroom on Sunday morning, it changed abruptly off from English into unintelligible sounds resembling a foreign tongue, and which, had I not been, as I think, pretty level-headed at the time, I should have construed as a mental state pathognomonic of mania. And yet I was not sufficiently 'at myself' to immediately seize pencil and pad and write down the sounds. When I subsequently asked of the psycho-automatism for a translation, among others I received . . . two."[1] The implication was that he was speaking a language he had known in a previous existence. This for a time he

[1] A. LeBaron, "A case of psychic automatism, including speaking with tongues." *Proc. of Society for Psychic Research*, 12, p. 289.

believed. The following is an example of a message in an unknown tongue and its purported translation:

"*The Unknown Tongue.*—Te rumete tau. Ilee lete leele luto scele. Impe re scele lee luto. Onko keere scete tere lute. Ombo te scele te bere te kure. Sinte te lute sinte Kuru. Orumo imbo impe rute scelete. Singe, singe, singe, eru. Imba, Imba, Imba.

"*The Translation.*—The old word! I love the old word of the heavens! The love of the heavens is emperor! The love of the darkness is slavery! The heavens are wise, the heavens are true, the heavens are sure. The love of the earth is past! The king now rules in the heavens!"[1]

The following is a portion of a poem given by the automatic voice, with its translation similarly given:

> "Ede pelute kondo nedode
> Igla tepete kompto pele
> Impe odode inguru lalele
> Omdo resene okoro pododo
> Igme odkondo nefulu kelala
> Nene pokonto sefo lodelu
> Impe telala feme olele
> Igde pekondo raog japate
> Rele pooddo ogsene ly mano."

"I have been looking, looking for daylight.
    Ages have flown and the years have grown dark;

[1] A. LeBaron, *op. cit.*, p. 290.

Over the hilltops the sun is now shining,
   Far from the sky comes the song of the lark.

Beauty is dawning, the darkness is passing,
Far up the vales fly the songs of the light.
Into the cities the joy will be spreading,
Into the by-ways the light will be spread;
Glory has come to the lost son of man!"[1]

Mr. LeBaron spent a great deal of time and energy trying to identify the language, but without much success. Of this he says, "I could not, and did not substantiate the verbiage as an actual language, although I could trace out a very large number of words in actual use among the non-Aryan tribes."[2]

Concerning the explanation of speaking with tongues, he says,

"In the attempt subsequently to explain the foregoing 'foreign tongues' I arranged nine different theories from which the reader may take his choice.

"*First Theory.* The sentences are all the work of a powerful unconscious imagination, and the sentences do not possess the natural consonantal and vowel elements of a language at all.

"*Second Theory.* They are brand new ideas in old and foreign verbal husks, the forms of which were latent in the man's subconsciousness at birth.

[1] A. LeBaron, *op. cit.*, pp. 293 f.
[2] A. LeBaron, *op. cit.*, p. 295.

"*Third Theory*. The consonantal and vowel combinations are but the articulate shells of very ancient ideas latent in this man's subconsciousness at birth, but out of the shells of which the meanings have been eaten up or metamorphosed by some at present unknown law of mental evolution, but are not now to be considered as ideas at all.

"*Fourth Theory*. They are none of the foregoing, but are new and actual presentations of real and new ideas in a foreign tongue.

"*Fifth Theory*. They are none of the foregoing, but a ludicrous and silly mistake of the man's imagination allied to some species of humorous hallucination and are not to be considered seriously, or they are a perjury, or a ghastly jest, or a very profound mental trick, or the loose jargon of a maniac.

"*Sixth Theory*. They are none of the foregoing, but are a species of scientific telepathy, and the consonantal and vowel combinations come from some morally indifferent, sublimely good, or awfully naughty source, and which is subject to the will of the man.

"*Seventh Theory*. Notwithstanding he says he never knew or heard these consonantal and vowel combinations before he uttered them, he may be in some very mysterious way deceiving himself.

"*Eighth Theory*. That it may not be beyond human belief that he is unconsciously in possession of a similar principle or intuitive linguistic power said to be possessed at this day by the higher adepts of India, or the Grand Lama of Thibet, or the Rosicrucians, by the means of which an unknown language is spoken by purely intuitive processes unknown to the analysis of western mental philosophy.

"*Ninth Theory.* That these consonantal and vowel combinations and their intuitive vocal adjustments may be startling scientific hints of mental forces latent in everybody, and which if studied, generalised, verified, systematized, and seriously investigated by philosophers might prove of incalculable benefit to the human race, but which could find no encouragement for expression in the nineteenth century because of the fierce and mocking intolerance of the conservative dogmas of the age."[1]

These two somewhat remarkable cases are reported at length, but it should not be concluded that these are the only non-religious cases of speaking with tongues which are available. For example, A. Maeder[2] reports speaking with tongues in a case of paranoid type of dementia præcox. The patient had a new language to express the new ideas with which his abnormal state provided him. It was primarily his own language for himself. The writer calls

[1] A. LeBaron, *op. cit.,* pp. 292 f.
[2] A. Maeder, "La Langue d'un aliéné, analyse d'un cas de glossolalie," *Archives de psychologie,* March 1910.

particular attention to the emotional and infantile aspects of the case, which were both very well marked.

CHAPTER IX

PSYCHOLOGICAL EXPLANATION

WHATEVER may be predicated of the psychological conditions of speaking with tongues in the New Testament, it is evident that the experience since then may be classed as ecstasy or allied phenomena. In ecstasy there is a condition of emotional exaltation, in which the one who experiences it is more or less oblivious of the external world, and loses to some extent his self-consciousness and his power of rational thought and self-control. Some persons seem to have acquired the ability to enter this state voluntarily.

There has been scarcely a religious leader of whom we have record who did not have his moments of ecstasy. The external conditions connected with speaking with tongues are usually those found in extreme excitement such as revival experience, and the phenomena seldom if ever appear in solitude. This is due in part, at least, to the nature and supposed usefulness of the gift. It may show itself under the intense nervous strain following persecution, as in the case of the Little Prophets, or the excitement may be more or less artificially stimulated as in some modern examples.

The diagnosis of ecstasy does not go unchallenged.

Some think the symptoms resemble a partially developed catalepsy, or, at least, one form of catalepsy. Others, again, call it hysteria. There are certain phases of the phenomena which resemble each of these states, and other phases which are common to all. The rigidity of the body, which is a common but not an unfailing symptom of catalepsy, and which may also be present in ecstasy and hysteria, is not often seen in speaking with tongues. In catalepsy there is a suspension of sensation, in ecstasy sensation may be unnoticed on account of the attention paid to some dominant idea, and in hysteria sensations are likely to be exaggerated or falsely reported, so as to simulate the symptoms of various diseases. In catalepsy there is a loss of consciousness, in hysteria consciousness may be present all the time, and in ecstasy any degree of consciousness may be present, but in case of unconsciousness the subject afterward remembers visions or auditions experienced during the trance. Catalepsy shows a loss of volition, while hysteria and ecstasy lack normal self-control. The hysteric is most susceptible to various suggestions, while the ecstatic seems to be dominated by a central idea. All three show nervous instability, but the ecstatic is most liable to give vent to the emotional pressure in impassioned utterances and extravagant bodily movements, although in one form of catalepsy passionate exclamations are unconsciously uttered. In all forms of nervous instability females predominate, and in hysteria they are in the proportion of twenty females to one male. In modern speaking with tongues women are more numerous.

It can thus be seen why speaking with tongues is diagnosed by different individuals as one of these three states, and how difficult it is to be sure which one. Those who believe that it should be classed as catalepsy compare certain cases of religious exaltation found among women shut up in convents in the thirteenth, fourteenth, fifteenth, and sixteenth centuries. It is true they did not all speak with tongues, if, indeed, any of them did, but they portrayed abnormal mental states which at that time, as now, passed among the unlettered for inspiration. Chambers[1] cites from De Haen, the case of a child twelve years of age, who began a paroxysm by being cataleptic, and ended by reciting the metrical Protestant version of David's Psalms, saying her catechism with proof texts, and preaching a sermon on adultery.

One must recognize that in naming the state he does not thereby explain it. That is too old a fallacy to ensnare us in this generation. We may classify speaking with tongues as hysteria, catalepsy, or ecstasy: this but aids us in description, we must still account for it. We may use other words, and de-

---

[1] "Catalepsy," *Reynolds' System of Medicine*, p. 104.

scribe it in more modern terms, but we still have failed to present the cause back of it.

In terms more directly borrowed from the vocabulary of modern psychology, in considering speaking with tongues we have to do with a state of personal disintegration, in which the verbo-motive centers of the subject are obedient to subconscious impulses. This, however, does not help us much in our diagnosis, for all three mental states already designated are characterized by a disintegration of personality or, to use another term, a dissociation of consciousness. Inability to remember a name is a dissociation of consciousness, and is a most common experience. When disintegration becomes so severe that the subconsciousness is in control, we have an abnormal condition. When the subconsciousness concentrates its energy on one motor or sensory function, this is likely to attract attention. We find this last condition in speaking with tongues.

Moreover, when the subconsciousness has control, we witness phenomena which were formerly called "automatic," and which were then described as being independent of the conscious will. These automatisms are divided into two classes, the sensory and the motor. The former consist of visions, auditions, and other hallucinations which have been elaborated in the subconsciousness, and are experienced with all the force of external perception, so that the persons

experiencing them call them real. In motor automatisms the subject performs some action, as, for example, automatic writing, which is a common experience of certain unstable people. Speaking with
tongues comes under the class of motor automatisms
and is sometimes called "phonetic automatism" to
distinguish it from automatic writing, both of which
are called verbal automatisms. All automatisms, psychologically considered, are fundamentally equiva-
lent. They are closely related and form a group, the
unity of which should be recognized.

It is rarely that an individual presents only one
kind of automatic manifestation. If he speaks with
tongues, he is likely to have visions or to hear voices.
When expectation or suggestion is absent, and speaking with tongues results, then the reason why the
motor or active rather than the sensory or passive
form takes place is a mystery hidden in the nervous
system of the subject. Expectation is rarely absent,
for Christianity is a religion of expression, and particularly of oral expression. Some form of verbal
testimony is expected and frequently demanded. In
modern times, at least, expectation with its consequent suggestion is a factor which looms large. It is
not a general hope either, but a specific desire to imi-
tate Pentecost, and a belief that this signal blessing
which God vouchsafed to the early followers of Jesus
will not be denied them. Pentecostal bands and sects

have as their chief tenets the restoration of Pentecostal gifts, prominent among which is the gift of tongues. Add to these the excitement already referred to, and conditions are ripe for a manifestation. The suggestion and expectation divert the emotional discharge into channels of motor activity; except for this the discharge might well take a sensory form and show itself in a vision rather than in the motor form of speaking with tongues.

In conditions of instability, the subconsciousness has a tendency to bring to the surface normally regressive and concealed characteristics, in which emotional elements predominate. According to the Freudian theories these would be of childish origin. Speaking with tongues is a childish reaction, showing itself not only by its appearance among the most primitive and untrained in a community, but by its similarity to the reactions of children. Paul recognized this, for in the midst of his discussions of the subject (I Cor. 14: 20) he stopped to say, "Brethren, be not childish in mind." Some would go so far as to trace the development of this manifestation in the individual so as to make it correspond with the development of talking in a child: first, the inarticulate sounds; second, the articulate sounds; and third, coined words which children frequently use in a language or at least in certain phrases which they have manufactured. There is another childish trait in speaking with tongues, that of being different, or at least superior to others,—and the glossolalics of the New Testament certainly thought themselves such. Speaking with tongues was a distinction and had the appearance, if not the thought, of, "I can do something that you cannot do." The glossolalic was distinctive, and some at Corinth, as well as some since that time, considered themselves especially blessed of God in the gift.

Lombard[1] calls attention to the fact that the gospel, in exercising powerful suggestions of conversion, called into being emotional tendencies ordinarily repressed or lying in a potential state, now known as complexes, and observes that there is nothing more favorable to the growth of automatic phenomena than those innermost agitations. This we now know to be true, and the influence and elaborations of this subject are now common. The disorganization due to religious gatherings of an emotional nature may have opposite effects. In some cases we may see the beginning of a superior reorganization, which commences with conversion, and is shown at first by startling psychological experiences, but is consummated in a well-ordered and well-balanced, clean life. At other times automatic actions of various kinds result from disorganization, actions which apart from some artificial influence seem to

[1] E. Lombard, *De la Glossolalie, etc.*, pp. 142 ff.

have no distinct religious value. Paul seemed to have placed the proper value on each, and although he experienced automatisms in visions and in speaking with tongues, he placed the emphasis upon the religious life.

It has been opined that there was a suggestion made to the early apostles that to talk to God or about Him required a language different from the common one, and that speaking with tongues was a subconscious attempt to supply this. We know the reverence in which the name of God was held, and even to-day we find some preachers who use different tones of voice in a religious service. We must realize that speaking with tongues was not initiated at Pentecost, but that similar if not identical experiences were known among the Hebrews as well as among other peoples. In Christianity, however, there was the strong emphasis upon the convert's being a new creature, and this might well presuppose a new language. The convert often took a new name, and new thoughts might seem to need new words. There were times in the lives of the ecstatics when ordinary words would seem inadequate to express their religious experiences, and when new words or a new language would seem necessary. Because that which is divine was considered incomprehensible and unintelligible to human beings, it was thought that a language challenging human understanding would be the one in which divine thought might be best expressed.

Not only is the language automatic but it is unintelligible. It is a foreign language in so much as it is usually foreign to the conscious personality of him who speaks, for like all automatisms the subject is unaware of it. In most cases of speaking with tongues the language is also unintelligible to the observers. To Paul this was objectionable, but some later writers considered it valuable as a sign. On the occasion of the incomprehensible and tumultuous manifestations in Irving's church, he wrote that without the character of incomprehensibility, which is always a feature of speaking with tongues, nothing would prove that it is really the Holy Spirit who speaks, and not a man. Pastor Paul said: "It is dangerous to have to express things that one comprehends. One is too easily inclined to mix in these his own thoughts. This can happen with the best intentions."

Mosiman,[1] in his explanation of the psychological conditions of speaking with tongues, identifies it with hypnotism, saying, "The ecstatic condition is really a hypnotic one." It is true that there are many common factors in the two states, and that ecstasy might be assigned to that group known as "auto-hypnotic," but to identify ecstasy and hypnotism is to carry the

[1] E. Mosiman, *Das Zungenreden, etc.*, pp. 101 ff.

analogy too far. We have in both states of insensibility, increased faculty of perception, ability to perform extraordinary physical feats, unusual power of endurance, apparent telepathy, etc., but in hypnotism we have the *rapport* with others, or at least with one other who gives suggestions, while in ecstasy we find an introverted consciousness more difficult to enter or influence than the most extreme case of ego-centric type of dementia præcox. It is also true that, as he points out, the conditions for bringing about the hypnotic state, namely, fixation of the attention, uniformity of perception, limitation of the power of the will, restriction of the field of consciousness, and suppression of ideas, are present in the modern Pentecostal meetings, but these usually bring about a condition for mob action rather than for hypnotism, which is an individual condition. The mastery of the subconsciousness and the abnormal suggestibility with lack of *rapport* are noticeable factors of common sleep, the lack of *rapport* being the chief difference between sleep and hypnotism; we could, therefore, connect ecstasy more intimately with sleep than with hypnotism, especially that form of sleep known as somnambulism. The dissociation of the consciousness and subconsciousness, and the post hypnotic suggestion, common to both hypnotism and sleep, are also prominent in ecstasy. I am not sure but that the term "ecstasy" has been used too loosely and too comprehensively, and that a more strict delimitation of its meaning and field should be made in the interest of science.

In the modern Pentecostal meetings there is another element which is also necessary to successful sleep or hypnotism, and that is the emphasis laid upon "yielding oneself." When this is accomplished, suggestion has full sway, and the higher, thinking, conscious personality gives way to the lower, reflexive, unconscious self. The effect of suggestion, however, may be considerably delayed. To accomplish this there are often days and nights of prayer and waiting, the vigil frequently being the one element necessary to establish the nervous condition upon which the ecstasy depends. Even then the ecstasy often begins with those who are abnormal—those particularly susceptible and suggestible—and spreads by the well-known laws of imitation and contagion, children and people of primitive qualities being the first to succumb.

Not infrequently twitchings, jerks, faintings, and other physical phenomena precede the tongues, and, as these are exceptionally contagious, people experiencing these are impressed with the fact that the tongues will follow. Mosiman condenses his psychological explanation of the phenomenon into the following: "The gift of tongues is an expression of thought and feeling by the speech-organs, which temporarily come under the control of the reflex nerve centers, the peculiar forms of which are determined by suggestion which chiefly consists of a verbal interpretation of the New Testament."

Those who speak with tongues are almost without exception devout, but ignorant and illiterate people. Many cultivated persons have longed and sought earnestly for the gift, but without avail. Irving, for example, never spoke with tongues, although he considered it a great favor, which for some reason was withheld from him. It was among the uncultivated portion of his congregation that the manifestation broke forth. To quote from a previous chapter concerning the experience among the Mormons, it was said: "Those who speak in tongues are generally the most illiterate among the 'Saints,' such as cannot command words as quick as they would wish, and instead of waiting for a suitable word to come to their memories they break forth in the first sound their tongues can articulate, no matter what it is."

Let us suppose, then, conditions as already described: external and internal excitement, suggestion in some form, and an illiterate person about to speak. *Ex hypothesi,* the person has poor power of expression and a limited vocabulary. The excitement drives him to say something. Perhaps for a short time he speaks normally, then the pressure of nervous energy increases, so that with the inadequate power of expression he is unable to say what he desires; confusion reigns in the mind; the upper centers become clogged, rational control takes flight, the lower centers assume control, a trance condition may be present, the suggestion is for speech, and because there is no rational control or direction there breaks forth a lot of meaningless syllables. When this gibberish cannot be understood, it is supposed by the hearers to be words of another language which is spoken by other people, and when the speaker disclaims all responsibility for the speech, as indeed he must if it originates in the subconsciousness and not in the consciousness, it is therefore supposed to be of divine origin. The clogging of the upper centers, as in speaking with tongues, is the opposite of stage fright, for in the latter condition it is the lower centers which are clogged, the upper centers continuing to function.

The outward expression of speaking with tongues may be one of three kinds, which are really three degrees of a progression which goes from the more remote forms to the nearer and more familiar forms of what we call organized language or speech. These are (1) inarticulate sounds, (2) articulate sounds which simulate words, and (3) fabricated or coined words. In addition to these related and progressive forms there is a fourth form, which is the actual

169

speaking of some words in a foreign tongue; but the language is always one with which the subject has come in contact, even if he can consciously speak no words in that language.

(1) Inarticulate sounds, imperfect utterances, or some other simple, vocal sounds are recognized in many glossolalics, especially at the beginning of their automatism. At times the whole phenomenon reduces itself to these inarticulate expressions, which, however, may also be the prelude to ecstatic prophecy. There are some individuals who do not go beyond this premonitory stage. It would be difficult, if not impossible, to organize or to bring under a uniform psychological interpretation the numerous examples of vocal utterances which precede the articulate speaking or at times replace it. They consist of cries, hiccoughs, sighs, murmurs, wailings, and even whistlings and grinding of teeth. In Carlyle's report of Irving's meeting he says that the glossolalics say mostly "ahs" and "ohs."

It seems that in a number of cases the subconsciousness of the subject had in some way to make a trial of its work. Even prior to the expression of sounds, several glossolalics testify that the preliminary signs of speaking with tongues are involuntary movements of the jaw without the emission of any sound. A great number of these *preglossolalic* manifestations present a peculiarly discordant character, which appears in connection with the special difficulty which the phonetic apparatus finds in adapting itself to the exigencies of automatic speech. Sometimes these may be the result of habit, expressing disapproval of what is going on or has gone on immediately before, but evidently they are forms due to excitement.

These preglossolalic sounds are recognized by some leaders of the tongues movement as a natural beginning. Mosiman says: "When a woman in the assembly only stammered, I heard the leader say, 'It will come all right. Thus the Holy Spirit begins; it will soon be able to make use of her better!'"[1] This development from inarticulate sounds to an articulate language may be either conscious and voluntary or unconscious and involuntary, and judging from other and similar experiences it would seem that more frequently it is the latter. Between these cases of simple excitement and the cases when the invasion of all the field of consciousness by a joyous or painful emotion manifests itself under the form of vocal reflexes, there exist so many degrees and shades that it is practically impossible to fix the limits.

Many Christians have groanings over their transgressions—very appropriate groanings—without going past the limits of conscious action. Nevertheless,

[1] Mosiman, *ibid.*, p. 111.

under the influence of contemplation, auto-hypno-
tization, or of the mental contagion, so frequent in
religious assemblies, it happens that the idea of sin
is reduced entirely to the idea, or rather the image,
of sadness, which in turn becomes almost, if not
quite, synonymous with physical suffering. Likewise
the joy of salvation and of divine adoption can become for the convert, who abandons himself, an intense feeling of well-being, an impression of joy, of
fulness, of harmony, which gives place to appropriate phonetic utterances. Perhaps we may say that
in its manifestations, speaking with tongues repre-
sents an attempt to restore the human word to a
new affective basis. The first appearance of the gift
in some, then, is possibly the result of a mere excess
of feeling, which expresses itself in uncontrolled utterances. With some it develops no further, others
consciously or unconsciously receive the suggestion
that a new and strange language is to be uttered, and
the subconsciousness begins and continues to produce syllables which sound like a real language.

When we consider the very close relation or even
identity between those termed "the spiritual" and
"the glossolalics," keeping in mind this form of inarticulate utterance which at times is preglossolalic
and at other times seems to be the whole content of
the experience, we wonder if Paul in Rom. 8: 26 did
not have some reference to this form when he said,

"For we know not how to pray as we ought; but the Spirit himself maketh intercessions for us with groanings which cannot be uttered."

(2) Pseudo language, or articulate sounds which simulate words, is probably the most common kind of speaking with tongues. It is this form which we have already cited as a typical example of speaking with tongues. It is evidently the variety to which Paul refers in Corinthians, and because of its having no meaning to it, it is naturally not understood and is consequently mistaken for a foreign language. Why speaking with tongues should develop in this particular form originally it is difficult to say.

With the great excitement attending certain experiences, we can well understand from other cases how the rational part of the mind—consciousness— would be put out of action; but in cases of this kind usually some habitual words, or, at least, some words suited to the particular emotion would be spoken, but they would be real words. If there were foreigners present and there were a desire—unexpressed wish—to communicate with them, or if there were a tradition or a prophecy to the effect that the inspired could communicate with strangers, then this would act as a suggestion, and the meaningless combination of syllables would result. According to the account in the second chapter of Acts, Peter thinks of this phenomenon as a fulfilling of the prophecy of Joel.

But the desire to speak to foreigners would give us a product similar to this form of speaking with tongues. If children in their play attempt to speak a foreign language, the result is always a meaningless combination of English syllables, if English is the ordinary language of the children.

After the experiences of New Testament times, especially when such expressions were supposed to be a particular and peculiar mark of approval of God and a gracious gift of the Holy Spirit, the suggestion would inevitably come to the spiritually exalted, and this pseudo-language would result. It would be difficult to conceive of a stronger suggestion. We cannot include in this such experiences as those among the Mormons in the later years. The leader of the meeting simply called upon some brother to speak with tongues. There would be no excitement, and the person addressed would arise and in a perfectly cool manner speak syllables which had no meaning in English, although they were English syllables.

A noteworthy characteristic of the verbatim examples of speaking with tongues already presented is the alliteration and repetition. Note such examples as these: "prou pray praddey," "pa palassate pa pau pu pe," "teli terattate taw," "terrei te te-te-te," "vole virte vum." We find this also in the case of LeBaron; the unknown tongue is expressed in such syllables as follow: "elee lete leele luto," "singe sirge singe," "imba imba imba." If one will voluntarily try to speak some unknown language he will recognize the tendency to alliteration and repetition. It is difficult to avoid it. It reminds us of the nonsense syllables used by children in their counting-out games, as, e.g., "Enee menee minee mo," which undoubtedly was originally an effort to speak in an unknown tongue.

It must be noted, however, that occasionally the claim is made that the language spoken is not supposed to be one which can be recognized, nor indeed an earthly language at all, but is a divine language known only to God and given by Him to specially favored persons for worship.

(3) Manufactured or coined words are a less common, but no less real form of speaking with tongues. Perhaps the most thoroughly investigated case is that of Hélène Smith, an epitome of which has already been given. To be sure this is not a case of religious speaking with tongues, but it is so closely connected as to be valuable as an illustration, for similar results are usually found in ecstatic religious experiences. To the alienist, speaking in tongues is not unfamiliar. Sometimes during an illness persons use an invented name for certain articles, and on recovery return to the common name again. Altogether, examples of a fabricated language are not

uncommon and are found in general abnormal states perhaps more often than in religious ecstasy.

In other forms of speaking with tongues, when a foreign language is actually spoken, the psychological explanation is that of exalted memory, due to the abnormal condition of the individual. Had we not authentic cases which show the possibility of such a thing, it would be scarcely credible that a person could reproduce foreign languages when consciously he knew not a word. There are such cases as that reported by Coleridge of the illiterate serving maid, who, in her delirium, repeated long passages of Latin, Greek, and Hebrew. Investigation showed that the only possibility of her having come in contact with these languages was during her service in the home of a clergyman. When she swept out his study in the morning the clergyman paced up and down the hall repeating passages in these languages. These were recorded, but normally could not be reproduced. It required the abnormal conditions to produce them.

A case is given by Abercrombie[1] which also shows the possibility of memory under abnormal conditions. "A girl of seven years, employed in tending cattle, slept in an apartment next to one occupied by an itinerant fiddler, a musician of considerable skill, who frequently spent the night in performing

[1] *Intellectual Powers of Man*, p. 304.

pieces of a refined description. She fell ill, was taken care of by a lady, and eventually became her servant. Some years elapsed, and the family were often surprised to hear music during the night. At length the sound was traced to the sleeping-room of the girl, who, fast asleep, was warbling in a manner exactly resembling the sweetest tones of a small violin. It was found that after being two hours in bed she became restless and began to mutter to herself; then, uttering noises resembling the tuning of a violin, she dashed off, after some prelude, into elaborate pieces of music, which she performed in a clear and accurate manner. A year or two passed away, and she began to vary her performance by imitating the sounds of an old piano in the house, the singing of the inmates; and further on she began to discourse on a variety of topics. The justness and truth of her remarks on all subjects excited the utmost astonishment in those who were acquainted with her limited means of acquiring information. She was known to conjugate correctly Latin verbs, and to speak several words in French. During her paroxysms it was almost impossible to awaken her, and when her eyelids were raised, and a candle brought near the eye, she seemed insensible to light. When about sixteen years of age she began to observe those who were in the apartment and answered questions put to her with astonishing acuteness. This affection went on for ten or eleven years. She was, when awake, a dull, awkward girl, slow in receiving any kind of instruction, without any talent for music, or apparently any recollection of what passed in her sleep. At the age of twenty-one she became immoral and was dismissed. It is believed that she afterwards became insane." The Little Prophets spoke correct French, Hélène Smith spoke Sanscrit.

With one or two exceptions the foreign languages produced have been but scraps picked up, and if heard in a religious service would be of a religious character. Care must be taken in the consideration of reports of persons talking Chinese, for example, that the report is given by someone who knows Chinese; or else it simply means that the utterance is something no one present understands, and probably that no one living could understand. We have already quoted Meyer as follows: "The sudden communication of the gifts of foreign languages is neither psychologically possible nor logically and morally conceivable." Is this going too far? If a strange tongue is heard, and the ecstatic has had no possible opportunity to hear this language at any time, then, so far as all investigations can prove, the hearing has been an illusion.

Mosiman[1] has traced many supposed examples of

[1] *Ibid.*, pp. 118 ff.

real speech in foreign languages, but has failed to discover an authentic case. He says: "In the examination of the gift of tongues no one has succeeded in finding a use for unknown foreign languages. During the Irvingianic movement the expressions of Mary Campbell were taken down and sent to recognized linguists, but they could discover no language. Dr. Tissot, a famous professor of medicine, examined the glossolalia at Morzines. He thought that the girls would have been able to have learned the German words from the Swiss cantons where German was spoken, and the Latin from its use in the church. With respect to the Arabic language, he found that the many wonderful examples were at once limited, and there was not much proof for it, for he could find no one who could speak or understand Arabic. In many places where I visited assemblies it was asserted that they spoke German, yet I have never heard a German word there. Others who investigated the gift of tongues in Chicago have made the same discovery. I have tried to investigate some of the 'wonderful' cases with which I was acquainted, and I have found no one who was noticeable as an example of the use of strange tongues. I asked one of the two women if Mr. D. had really spoken German. She told me that she had heard only four words: 'Jesus Christ kommt bald.' That is, however, an entirely usual thought among the speakers in tongues,

and many of the adherents who heard Mr. D. are
Germans. It might have been psychologically possible that Mr. D. used this expression, but it is more
probable that the expression came from the imagination of the hearers. Also in the account which the
Chicago daily paper reports there is little else. The
lady who had gone to a Chinese with the girl told
me that he had understood the girl, but the Chinese
was no more to be found. It also resulted that it had
been proposed by someone else, and not by the girl
herself, to go to a Chinese laundry to speak with a
Chinese. I sent the script to a Chinese missionary in
Chicago, and he found no Chinese characters, but
thought that the writing might be like the Japanese.
I wrote to the editor of the paper which reported
the account of the gift of tongues in Pittsburgh and
received the following answer: 'The brothers and
sisters are called McGuire and they live somewhere
here in the city, but I have not the address. I meet
them now and then in the assembly, but I have not
seen them in a few weeks. They are, however, trust-
worthy people.' The other questions which I asked
were overlooked. From the missionaries who heard
Chinese spoken I received the answer: 'Here in the
congregation there are often proclamations made
that are considered Chinese. Except in one case we
have never recognized words which we have understood. In this case there were some sentences which

were understood by Mrs. K. and they were rightly translated when the announcement was interpreted.' As far as I know there is no case of speaking in strange tongues which has been strictly and scientifically investigated that cannot be explained by recognized psychological laws. If we also do not judge as strictly as Meyer, we are not entitled to deny also the assertion of Dr. Sidis that 'one cannot speak a foreign language the words of which one has never heard.' "

Perhaps we should not terminate this discussion without paying brief attention to the so-called "interpretation of tongues," which Paul recognized as a spiritual gift, but which he always placed last on the list. Where the "gift" is not pure fraud, it is undoubtedly the result of suggestion which the subconsciousness receives and acts upon. Mosiman opines that it "seems to demand the powers of thought-reading," but that seems to suppose that the interpretation of tongues is a genuine interpretation of the ecstatic utterances of the speaker, or at least the real expression in well-known language of the thoughts which the speaker is trying to express in unknown tongues. Nothing in the investigations of modern examples seems to justify this. Nothing in the interpretation seems to bear any relation to the unknown tongues, except that occasionally a syllable of the unknown tongues may suggest the sound of a certain word in the known tongue and the interpretation is built around this. Let us recall the example of the Mormon boy, given on a previous page, who had some skill in interpretation. When called upon to interpret the exclamation of a woman who arose in meeting and said: "Omela, meli, melee," the boy promptly interpreted as follows: "Oh! my leg! my thigh! my knee!"

As a matter of fact the interpretation of tongues has little standing either religiously or psychologically, and is neither emphasized nor valued as is the speaking with tongues. The speaking in tongues is an end in itself, its very unintelligibility satisfying the psychological craving for extraordinary expression and the religious craving for proof of inspiration and the direct action of God; but interpretation, while undoubtedly at times the result of ecstasy as in the speaking with tongues, is a relative, and frequently an artificial, experience. In the nature of the case the interpretation often comes as an answer to prolonged prayers and anticipation attracting the results of the suggestion of New Testament experiences as well as of suggestions which inevitably cling to the experiences in the speaking with tongues.

At Corinth, according to Paul, as well as in modern times, the glossolalic may also be the interpreter. He says (I Cor. 14: 15), "Greater is he that prophesies than he that speaketh with tongues, except he interpret." Rev. Mr. Sheat[1] tells how he became an interpreter after having received the gift of tongues. " 'In the night I awakened from my sleep and commenced to pray to obtain the gift of interpretation. After some words of prayer I was seized by the same intense force that I had felt in me the preceding days, and it was under the action of this force that I continued in prayer. . . . In about one hour, I apprehended how one succeeds in interpreting. One word was given me in a foreign tongue, and its translation in English followed immediately. Then the two were repeated, which pointed clearly that they signified the same thing. Since then, when someone speaks in tongues, the interpretation comes to me as soon as I seek it.' "

In the case of Hélène Smith it was somewhat similar. Evidently LeBaron's interpretation came as a whole after the glossolalic passage was concluded, whether of prose or poetry. In many passages both in Mlle. Smith's and in LeBaron's translations the same word is always translated the same way, and there is an evident endeavor to simulate a true language with grammatical forms, Mlle. Smith's being distinctly French. The experience of speaking with tongues and that of interpretation are psychologically not very different, as both are the result of the

---

[1] Quoted by Lombard, pp. 181 f.

subconsciousness acting in ecstasy, but the interpretation carries with it a larger amount of suggestive material.

BIBLIOGRAPHY

Abercrombie, J. *Inquiries concerning the intellectual powers of Man and the investigations of truth.* New York, 1853.

Abrams, M. "Baptism of the Holy Spirit at Mukti." *Missionary Review,* 19 (n.s.): 619. Aug. 1906.

American Society of Church History. *Papers,* Vol. II, Pt. I: 19.

Anguetil, L. P. *Vie du Maréchal de Villars.* Vol. I. Paris, 1784.

Baird, H. M. "The Camisard Uprising, etc." *Paper of American Society of Church History,* Vol. II, Pt. I.

Barde, E. "La glossolalie," *Revue de theologie et des questions religieuses.* 5: 125-138.

Baxter, R. *Narrative of facts characterizing the supernatural manifestations, in members of Mr. Irving's congregation.* London, 1833.

Beadle, J. H. *Life in Utah, mysteries and crimes of Mormonism.* Philadelphia, National Pub. Co., 1870.

Bennett, W. J. E., ed. *The church's broken unity—on Presbyterianism and Irvingism.* London, Hayes, n.d.

Braithwaite, W. C. *Beginnings of Quakerism.* London, Macmillan, 1912.

Bray, A. E. *Revolt of the Protestants of the Cevennes.* London, Murray, 1870.

Butler, A. *Lives of the Saints,* 4 vols. London, 1756-59.

Clemen, C. "The 'Speaking with Tongues' of the early Christians." *Expository Times,* 10: 344.

Davenport, F. M. *Primitive traits in religious revivals.* London, Macmillan, 1905.

Encyclopedia Britannica. "Tongues, Gift of." Article.

Felice, G. de. *History of the Protestants of France.* Trans. Barnes. London, 1853.

Flournoy, Th. *Des Indes à la Planète Mars. (From India to the Planet Mars.)* Geneva, 1900.

Franklin, B. *Works.* Ed. by J. Bigelow, Vol. I.

Froude, J. A. *Thomas Carlyle: a history of his life in London,* II. New York, Harpers, 1885.

"Gift of tongues in the ancient church." *Prospective Review.* 8: 303.

Görres, J. J. *La Mystique divine, naturelle, et diabolique.* Trans. from the German by C. Sainté-Foi. Paris, Poussielque-Rusand, 1862.

Gould, S. B. *Virgin saints and martyrs.* New York, Crowell, 1923.

Green, D. "Gift of tongues." *Bibliotheca Sacra.* 22: 99.

Gunnison, J. W. *The Mormons or Latter Day Saints in the Valley of the Great Salt Lake, etc.* Philadelphia, Lippincott, 1860.

Hammond, W. A. *Spiritualism and allied causes and conditions of nervous derangement.* New York, Putnam, 1876.

Haskett, W. J. *Shakerism unmasked.* Pittsfield, Walkley, 1828.

Hastings, J., ed. *Dictionary of the Bible.* 4: 793. New York, Scribners, 1909.

Hastings, J., ed. *Encyclopedia of Religion and Ethics.* 3: 368. New York, Scribners, 1908.

Hawthornthwaite, S. *Mr. Hawthornthwaite's adventures among the Mormons as an elder during eight years.* Manchester, England, 1857.

Hayes, D. A. *The gift of tongues.* New York, Eaton and Main, 1913.

Heath, R. "The little prophets of the Cevennes." *Contemporary Review*, 49: 117. January 1886.

Henke, F. G. "Gift of tongues and related phenomena at the present day." *American Journal of Theology*, 13: 193.

Inglis, J. "Gift of tongues: another view." *Theological Monthly*, 5: 425.

Intercessory Missionary. Fort Wayne, Ind.

Irving, Edward. "Interpretation of tongues," in his *Collected Writings*. Vol. V. London, Strahan, 1866.

Jurieu, P. *Lettres pastorales adresses aux fidèles de France*. Rotterdam, 1686-87. English translation, 1689.

Kempmeier, A. "Recent parallels to the miracle of Pentecost." *Open Court*, 22: 492.

Kennedy, J. H. *Early days of Mormonism*. Scribners, New York, 1888.

Lamson, D. R. *Two years experience among the Shakers . . . a condensed view of Shakerism as it is*. Lamson, W. Boyston, 1848.

LeBaron, A., pseud. "A case of psychic automatism, including speaking with tongues." Society for Psychical Research, *Proceedings*, XII: 277.

Lombard, E. *De la Glossolalie chez les premiers chrètiens et des phénomènes similaires*. Bridel, Lausanne, 1910.

McClintock, J., and Strong, J. *Cyclopædia of Biblical, theological and ecclesiastical literature*. 10: 479. New York, 1869-81.

Maeder, A. "La Langue d'un Aliéné, analyse d'un cas de glossolalie," *Archives de Psychologie*, March 1910.

Marion, E. *La Theatre Sacré des Cevennes*. London, 1707.

Meyer, H. A. W. *Critical and exegetical commentary on the New Testament*. "Acts." Edinburgh, 1873-83.

Middleton, C. *Introductory discourse and the free inquiry into miraculous powers.* London, 1749.

Mosiman, E. *Das Zungenreden, geschichtlich und psychologisch untersucht.* Mohr, Tübingen, 1911.

Nevius, J. L. *Demon possession and allied themes.* Revell, New York, 1896.

Newbold, W. R. "Spirit writing and 'speaking with tongues.' " *Popular Science Monthly,* 49: 508.

Oliphant, Mrs. M. O. *The life of Edward Irving.* Hurst and Blacketts, London, n.d.

Peebles, J. M. *The demonism of the ages and spirit obsession.* Peebles, Battle Creek, 1904.

Pentecost Evangel, The. Springfield, Mo.

Perkins, J. E. *The Brooding Presence and Pentecost.* Gospel Publishing House, Springfield, Mo., 1926.

Peyrat, N. *Histoire des Pasteurs du Desert, etc.* M. Aurel Frères, Paris, 1842.

Pierson, A. T. "Speaking with tongues." *Missionary Review,* 20: 487, 682.

Pilkington, G. *The unknown tongues discovered to be English, Spanish, and Latin; the Rev. Edward Irving proved to be erroneous in attributing their utterance to the influence of the Holy Spirit.* London, 1831.

Roberts, A., and Donaldson, J. *Ante Nicene Fathers.* Edinburgh, 1870-77.

Schaff, P. *History of the Apostolic Church.* Scribners, New York, 1853.

Schaff, P. *History of the Christian Church.* Scribners, New York, 1882-1910.

Seddon, A. E. "Edward Irving and unknown tongues." *Homiletic Review,* 57: 103.

Shaftesbury, Earl of. *Characteristics of men, manners,*

opinions, times. "Letter concerning Enthusiasm, to my Lord Sommers." I. London, 1737.

Simmons, J. P. *History of tongues.* Frostproof, Florida.

Smiles, S. *The Huguenots in France.* Daldy, Isbister and Co., London, 1875.

Stead, W. T. *History of the Welsh Revival.* Pilgrim Press, Boston, 1905.

Stevens, A. *The History of Methodism.* Philips and Hunt, New York, 1858.

Walker, D. *The gift of tongues.* Clark, Edinburgh, 1906.

Wesley, J. *Works,* Vol. V. Harper, New York, 1826-27.

White, A. *Demons and tongues.* The Pentecostal Union, Bound Brook, N. J., 1910.

White, A. D. *History of the warfare of science with theology in Christendom.* Appleton, New York, 1896.

Wright, A. "Gift of tongues: a new view." *Theological Monthly,* 5: 161, 272.

Wright, A. *Some New Testament problems.* Methuen, London, 1898.

Zaugg, E. H. *A genetic study of the spirit phenomena in the New Testament.* Private ed., Chicago, 1917.

INDEX

191

CPSIA information can be obtained at www.ICGtesting.com
Printed in the USA
245445LV00003B/82/P